TOKYO TRAVEL GUIDE 2024

SAVE MONEY AND EXPERIENCE AUTHENTIC CITY LIFE WITH TIPS ON BUDGET HOTELS & MUST-SEE SIGHTS

HANA TAKASHIRO

HANA TAKASHIRO

CONTENTS

The information provided in this travel guide is intended solely for general guidance and informational purposes to enhance your experience and understanding of the destination. Although every effort has been made to ensure accuracy and reliability, the author assumes no responsibility for errors, omissions, or any unforeseen changes in information such as addresses, hours, or prices.

Please remember that travel experiences may vary, and it is recommended to verify details with relevant authorities or service providers before making final arrangements. The author is not liable for any travel issues, safety incidents, or inconveniences arising from the use of this guide. Readers should exercise personal judgment and consider local laws, customs, and health recommendations.

Any actions you take based on the content of this guide are strictly at your own risk.

INTRODUCTION

Tokyo is Japan's capital and one of the most important cities in the world, both economically and culturally. It's located on Japan's eastern coast, facing the Pacific Ocean, with South Korea, China, and Russia across the sea. Over 37 million people live in its greater metro area, and you'll see why Tokyo has such a big pull: this city mixes ancient traditions with high-tech everything, and it's the heart of Japanese culture, finance, and tech.

The currency here is the **Japanese Yen (¥)**, and you can easily find ATMs in convenience stores like 7-Eleven and in all train stations. Tokyo's public transportation system is extensive, fast, and clean. You'll mainly use **rechargeable Suica or Pasmo cards**, which work on trains, buses, and even at vending machines and some stores. The **JR Yamanote Line** is the loop line connecting major neighborhoods like Shibuya, Shinjuku, and Ueno, while the **Tokyo Metro** gets you to spots that aren't on the Yamanote Line, like Asakusa and Ginza.

The economy is massive, with the **Tokyo Stock Exchange** being one of the largest in the world. The city is home to big companies like Sony, Toyota, and Honda, making it a global leader in electronics, robotics, and automotive technology. Tokyo's **GDP alone rivals that of some entire countries**, making it not just Japan's economic center but a major player worldwide.

The history goes back hundreds of years, starting as a fishing village called Edo. It became the seat of the powerful Tokugawa shogunate in the 1600s, which turned it into Japan's political center. Over the years, Tokyo faced fires, earthquakes, and bombings during WWII, but it rebuilt every time, growing stronger.

Today, it's a model of resilience and innovation, with skyscrapers that can withstand earthquakes and modern buildings mixed with traditional ones.

Each area of Tokyo has its own unique feel. The **east side, like Asakusa and Ueno**, keeps traditional Japan alive. In Asakusa, you'll find **Senso-ji Temple**, Tokyo's oldest, surrounded by old-style shops. **Ueno** is home to museums, Ueno Zoo, and a huge park filled with cherry blossoms in spring. The **west side, like Shibuya and Shinjuku**, is where Tokyo's fast-paced, modern energy comes alive. **Shibuya's scramble crossing** is one of the busiest in the world, surrounded by shopping and cafes. In Shinjuku, skyscrapers, nightlife, and endless dining options give you a true city vibe.

The influence on pop culture is huge. The city is the global center for **anime, manga, and gaming**. In **Akihabara**, the "electric town," you'll find shops dedicated to electronics, anime, and themed cafes, drawing fans from all over the world. Tokyo is also a major player in fashion; from **Harajuku's street style** to Ginza's high-end stores, the city sets trends globally.

Food here is top-notch, and Tokyo has more **Michelin-starred restaurants** than anywhere else. From sushi at the famous **Tsukiji Outer Market** to ramen shops and casual izakayas, Tokyo offers great food at every price. Many restaurants are small and focus on a few perfected dishes, so you're almost guaranteed a memorable meal, even in a tiny spot.

After hosting the **2020 Summer Olympics**, Tokyo continued to upgrade its infrastructure. The city added new spaces like the **New National Stadium** and redesigned green areas, making it one of the cleanest, most efficient cities you'll find. Projects like the **Midtown Garden Project** mix green rooftops and eco-friendly design, providing green spaces in the middle of the city's skyscrapers.

Around **15 million people visit Tokyo every year** to see its famous mix of old traditions and super-modern attractions. Most tourists spend between **$1,500 to $3,000** for a week, covering things like hotels, food, shopping, and tours. Tokyo's tourism brings in billions each year, and visitors keep coming because they can find **historic temples, futuristic tech, amazing food, and unique fashion** all in one city.

Some of biggest attractions are **Tokyo Tower** and **Tokyo Skytree**, both giving you amazing views of the city. **Shibuya Crossing** is one of the busiest intersections in the world, and **Senso-ji Temple** in Asakusa is Tokyo's oldest, giving a feel of traditional Japan. If you're into fashion, **Harajuku** is the place for unique, colorful styles, while **Akihabara** is paradise for anime and tech fans. Shinjuku has lively nightlife, Odaiba is known for its futuristic buildings, and the Imperial Palace has beautiful gardens that bring a bit of peace to the city.

The **weather** changes a lot by season. **Spring** (March-May) brings mild temperatures around 50-70°F. **Summer** (June-August) is hot and humid, often reaching 85°F or more, and it's festival season. **Fall** (September-November) has cooler weather and colorful leaves, while **winter** (December-February) is usually mild, though there's occasional snow.

People are known for being **polite, helpful, and respectful**. In public, you'll notice how everyone respects personal space, keeps noise down, and waits their turn. Locals are used to seeing tourists, especially in busy areas, so you'll find English signs in popular spots, though speaking a little Japanese goes a long way.

CHAPTER 1
WHY TOKYO IN 2024/2025?

Now, in the end of 2024/2025 is the year you want to visit because **new places have opened** and some amazing **events are happening**. The **Tokyo Contemporary Art Center** just opened, and it's not like other museums. You don't just look at the art—you move through it, interact with it, and experience it in a totally different way. It's full of cool tech mixed with Japanese tradition.

There's also **Shibuya Stream**, where you can put on a VR headset and travel through Tokyo's past and future in one experience. You'll see old Tokyo streets and futuristic skyscrapers in the same place, and it feels real. It's perfect if you're into tech or just want something different from your typical tourist spots.

If you like festivals, **the Tokyo Summer Festival 2024** is happening all across the city. You'll find live performances in places like **Ueno Park** and **Asakusa**, mixing traditional Japanese arts with modern music. You could walk from a quiet theater performance in the park to a DJ set in Shibuya that's combining electronic music with traditional Japanese instruments. And if you're into sports, the **Tokyo Marathon** is a huge event where runners take over the streets. The energy in the city during this time is incredible.

Hotels have also stepped up in 2024. **The Tokyo Edition Toranomon** is offering special experiences that include private tours of new attractions, like the re-designed **TeamLab Planets**. You get to skip the lines and go behind the scenes, making it more than just a place to sleep—it's a full-on luxury experience.

The city's also focusing on **green spaces**. You'll see new eco-friendly buildings, some of them with rooftop gardens where you can relax while looking at the city. **Midtown Garden Project** is one of the best spots for this. You sit surrounded by plants on a rooftop, with a view of the busy streets below, but it feels peaceful, almost like you're not even in the city.

2024 is also big for food. Restaurants like **Narisawa** are doing something new by blending French and Japanese cooking while using local, sustainable ingredients.

WHAT'S NEW IN THE WORLD'S LARGEST METROPOLIS?

The **Tokyo Contemporary Art Center** just opened, and it's not like any museum you've seen before.

Instead of just looking at art, you'll walk through it. The exhibits change with your movements. Lights, sounds, and images react to you, so every visit feels different. It's not just paintings or sculptures—**it's digital and interactive**, blending technology with traditional Japanese culture. If you want something fresh and unique, this is it.

Shibuya Sky is a new observation deck where you get **360-degree views** of the entire city.

On clear days, you'll even see **Mount Fuji**. It's super modern, with **LED light shows** in the evening. It's one of the best places to get an unforgettable view of the city, especially at night when everything lights up.

Another exciting spot is the **Tokyo Tower Digital Art Museum**.

Here, the art reacts to you. As you walk, the lights and projections change, making you feel like you're in a living, moving artwork. You're not just a visitor —you're part of the exhibit. It's an immersive experience, and the rooms look different depending on where you go, so it's always interesting.

If you're a foodie, **Sugalabo V** is the restaurant to try. It's different because there's no menu. The chef makes a custom meal based on the freshest ingredients available that day. It's small, exclusive, and hard to get into, but if you can, it's worth it. Each meal is unique, and it feels like a personal dining experience you won't forget.

In the **Tokyo Bay** area, new skyscrapers are going up like the **Ariake Garden Tower**, but they aren't just big buildings. They have **rooftop gardens** and green spaces, mixing nature into the urban environment. You can shop, eat, and even stay in luxury apartments all in one place, and it's built with sustainability in mind, making the area eco-friendly.

This year's **Tokyo Biennale** is a major art event where artists from around the world are creating public artworks. You'll see giant sculptures and murals in everyday places like **Asakusa** and **Shinjuku**. It turns the city streets into art galleries, and the installations are meant to surprise you as you walk around. It's like discovering art at every corner.

During **Roppongi Art Night**, the whole district turns into an art festival.

Buildings light up, and streets are filled with performances and art displays. The entire area becomes a massive art space, with exhibits everywhere, and the **buildings themselves are part of the show**. It's one night where the entire district feels alive with creativity and light.

TOP 5 INSIDER TIPS FOR FIRST-TIME VISITORS

Learn a few basic Japanese phrases to make things easier for yourself. Saying **"sumimasen"** (excuse me) when you need to get someone's attention or **"arigatou gozaimasu"** (thank you) will help a lot. Most people don't speak much English, especially in smaller shops or local restaurants. Download **Google Translate** and make sure to get the offline Japanese language pack. You can use it to translate menus, signs, or even have short conversations if you're stuck.

Before you go, download a few key apps. The **Japan Official Travel App** is great for navigating trains and public transport. It gives real-time schedules, platform numbers, and the fastest routes. Also, use **Google Maps**, but download offline maps for the areas you're visiting in case you lose signal. If you're booking places or want to chat with locals, having **LINE** will help—it's the main messaging app people use here, and some restaurants might use it for reservations.

It's important to know a bit about Japanese etiquette. On public transport, **stay quiet**—no phone calls or loud conversations, especially on trains. You'll also notice people line up neatly for buses and trains, so do the same. When you go to a restaurant, remember that **tipping isn't necessary**. If you leave money on the table, they'll probably run after you to give it back. At shrines or temples, follow the simple rules—bow before entering, wash your hands at the entrance fountains, and pray quietly.

When you're in crowded areas like **Shibuya Crossing** or **Shinjuku**, it's easy to get lost. If you do, look for a **koban** (a small police box). The police officers there are really helpful and used to giving tourists directions. Take a photo of your hotel's name and address in Japanese as soon as you check-in so you can show it to anyone if you need help getting back. This will be super useful for taxi drivers or locals who don't speak English.

Bring cash because **not everywhere takes credit cards**. While big stores and hotels are fine with cards, many small restaurants, street vendors, and attractions only accept cash. The best places to get cash are **7-Eleven ATMs** and **Post Office ATMs**, which work with international cards. Some other ATMs might not accept your card, so always keep some yen on hand for smaller purchases or meals.

CHAPTER 2
PLANNING ESSENTIALS

BEST TIME TO VISIT

SPRING: MARCH-MAY

Spring here is all about **cherry blossoms**—you'll see them blooming from late March to early April, turning everything pink and magical. People gather everywhere for **hanami**, which is more than just looking at flowers—it's an event.

You'll see groups of friends and families laying out their picnic blankets under the trees, sharing food and drinks. If you want to experience this, go to **Ueno Park**. The cherry trees there create these long tunnels of pink, and it's one of the most popular spots, so yes, it's busy, but that's part of the fun. You'll want to get there early if you want a good spot. If you can, stay until evening because the trees are lit up, and the whole park feels like a festival.

Another beautiful place for cherry blossoms is **Senso-ji Temple** in Asakusa. This place is stunning in spring. Imagine walking through this ancient temple, surrounded by sakura petals. It's a great spot to feel a mix of culture and nature all in one. While you're there, you can explore **Nakamise Street**, grab some traditional snacks, and really soak in the atmosphere. The combination of the blossoms and the historical setting is something you'll remember.

Spring is also festival season, with events like the **Sanja Matsuri** in May. This one takes over Asakusa, with portable shrines being carried through the streets. It's loud, packed, and full of energy. You'll see traditional outfits, hear drumming, and feel the excitement in the air. If you're around in mid-May, it's worth being part of this huge cultural event.

The **weather** in spring is perfect—mild days with temperatures around 10°C to 20°C (50°F to 68°F), which means you won't be sweating or freezing. It's a great time to walk around and explore without worrying about being too hot or cold. You'll need a light jacket for the evenings, though, especially early in the season.

If you're here for the **sakura**, be aware that the bloom only lasts about a week. Timing is everything. You'll want to check the **sakura forecast** before you go, so you can catch the blossoms at their peak. The timing shifts slightly every year depending on the weather, but late March is usually a safe bet. Make sure you plan ahead if you're visiting places like **Shinjuku Gyoen** or Ueno because these spots fill up fast, especially on weekends. Going early or on a weekday is the best way to avoid the big crowds.

SUMMER: JUNE-AUGUST

Summer here gets intense with **temperatures easily hitting above 30°C** and the humidity making it feel even hotter, especially in **July and August**. You'll notice the heat right away—there's no way around it. Walking a few blocks, you'll feel like you've been in the sun for hours, and the air feels thick. So, trust me, you'll want to have **water with you all the time**, and you'll be stopping at vending machines or convenience stores a lot just to stay cool. Everyone does it—you'll see locals grabbing cold drinks constantly because staying hydrated isn't an option, it's a must.

Before the full-on heat of July and August, **June** is the **rainy season**. It's unpredictable, and even when the day looks sunny, it can start raining out of nowhere. It's not torrential rain all day, but **sudden downpours** hit often in the afternoons. You'll notice locals always have umbrellas with them, especially those **clear plastic ones** you can pick up at any convenience store for just a few yen. You don't need to pack a raincoat—just grab an umbrella as soon as you arrive. The rain cools things down for a bit, but then the humidity comes right back, so you'll still feel the heat even after a quick shower.

Now, **summer is festival season**, and this is when the city really comes alive. The heat doesn't stop anyone, and it's the time for **Bon Odori**, which happens around **July or August** in different neighborhoods. This is a traditional dance festival where locals, dressed in **yukata** (a light summer kimono), dance in circles to the beat of taiko drums. You'll hear the music before you see the festival—just follow the sound, and you'll find groups of people all gathered around shrines or parks, dancing together. You don't need to know the steps—you can join in, follow the rhythm, and just enjoy the atmosphere. If you're near **Asakusa** or **Ueno**, you'll probably find a Bon Odori happening nearby. It's casual, laid-back, and honestly, the best way to experience local culture in a real, hands-on way. The food stalls set up around the festival will keep you well-fed, with plenty of snacks like **takoyaki** (octopus balls) and **yakitori** (grilled chicken skewers) to try.

Then there's the real summer spectacle: **fireworks**. The **Sumida River Fireworks** in late July is the biggest show of all. You're looking at **thousands of fireworks** lighting up the sky for hours, with huge crowds gathered along the riverbanks, rooftops, and any other space people can find. You can't just show up last minute—if you want a good view, you need to **arrive hours before**. The locals know this, and they bring full setups—**picnic blankets, food, drinks**, everything you need to settle in for a long evening waiting for the fireworks to start. The energy builds as the sun goes down, and by the time the fireworks begin, the entire place is buzzing. The display is massive, and it's one of those things you have to experience once because the sky lights up in ways you can't even imagine. If you're not around for Sumida, there are still smaller fireworks festivals throughout **early August**, like the **Tokyo Bay Fireworks**, which reflect off the water and create an incredible view.

But in all this excitement, the heat can sneak up on you. When you're outside for hours, especially at festivals or waiting for fireworks, make sure you're **drinking water all the time**. Grab a bottle from a vending machine or pick up **Pocari Sweat**, which is a Japanese sports drink that helps you stay hydrated when you're sweating. Trust me, you'll be sweating a lot. You'll also want to duck into **air-conditioned stores** when you can. Every **department store and mall** blasts their air conditioning, and it's a great way to cool down without losing any momentum in your day. Whether you're in between shopping or just exploring, stepping into the cool air is going to feel like a lifesaver.

Even with the heat, there's nothing like summer here. The festivals, fireworks, and atmosphere make it a time when the city feels fully alive. People are outside, even in the sweltering heat, enjoying the season, and the energy is contagious. You just have to be ready for it

AUTUMN: SEPTEMBER-NOVEMBER

Autumn is one of the best times to be here. The leaves turn bright **red, orange, and yellow**, and the whole city feels calmer. The weather stays nice, around **15°C to 20°C**, so you can walk around for hours without sweating or freezing. The best time to see the leaves is **mid-to-late November** when everything is in full color, but you can catch it from **late September through November**. The crowds are smaller than in spring, so it's perfect if you want to enjoy the scenery without pushing through tons of people.

The top spot to see the fall colors is **Rikugien Garden**. The trees around the pond are stunning, especially when they reflect in the water. You can walk around the garden, and if you go during the peak season, they light up the trees at night, making everything feel magical. Another good place is **Shinjuku Gyoen**. It's huge, and you'll see a lot of different trees, so the colors are all mixed together. You can wander for hours, and because it's so big, you'll always find a quiet spot.

There are also some cool **festivals** during autumn. The **Tokyo Jidai Matsuri** in **November** is a big parade where people dress up in traditional costumes, like samurai, and walk through **Asakusa**. It's like seeing history right in front of you, and the autumn colors make it even more special. In **October**, there's the **Oeshiki Festival** at **Ikegami Honmonji Temple**. It's quieter, but the temple is filled with glowing lanterns, and the procession feels really peaceful, especially with the cool autumn air.

Food is a big part of the season too. You'll see roasted **sweet potatoes** and **chestnuts** everywhere, especially at the food stalls during festivals. Restaurants also change their menus to focus on autumn ingredients like **mushrooms** and **root vegetables**, so it's a good time to try something new and seasonal.

WINTER: DECEMBER-FEBRUARY

Winter here completely changes the city's vibe, and one of the things you'll notice first is how the cold air sharpens everything, making even the most familiar streets feel different. If you're lucky, you might catch a light dusting of **snow**, which usually sticks around for a day or two before melting away, giving everything a magical touch. But even without snow, the **winter illuminations** will catch your attention immediately. These aren't just some simple lights—it's like the whole city gets dressed up in glowing displays that completely transform neighborhoods.

You've got to check out **Tokyo Midtown** in **Roppongi**. It's right in the heart of the city, and during winter, they cover the entire area with millions of LED lights, making the trees and streets shimmer. You can get there easily by taking the **Tokyo Metro Hibiya Line** or **Toei Oedo Line** to **Roppongi Station**, then it's just a short walk. The lights stretch all the way around **Midtown Garden** and **Hinokicho Park**, and if you go around sunset, you'll catch the lights turning on, which makes the whole place feel even more special. The display usually runs from **mid-November to early January**, so you have plenty of time to take it all in. Nearby, you can grab a bite at one of the fancy cafes or restaurants inside **Tokyo Midtown**—there's a wide range, from Japanese to Western, but expect to pay around **¥2,000 to ¥4,000** for a decent meal.

Another spot that's become super popular for winter illuminations is the **Shibuya Blue Cave**, located near **Shibuya Station**. You can get there easily by hopping on the **JR Yamanote Line** or **Tokyo Metro Ginza Line** to **Shibuya**, and from there, it's just a five-minute walk. The **Blue Cave** stretches along **Keyaki Namiki Street** and is famous for its tunnel of blue lights, which look absolutely surreal. You'll want to walk the whole stretch, take a ton of photos, and maybe stop for a warm drink at one of the nearby cafes. If you're feeling hungry, pop into one of the many ramen shops in Shibuya. You can get a hearty bowl of **ramen** for around **¥900 to ¥1,200**—perfect for warming up after being outside.

Marunouchi near **Tokyo Station** is another must-see spot, especially if you're into more elegant, understated illuminations. The **Naka-dori Street** in Marunouchi is lined with trees draped in warm white lights, which give the whole area a cozy, festive feel without being too flashy. It's easy to reach—just take the **JR Yamanote Line** to **Tokyo Station**, and it's about a 10-minute walk from there. What's cool about Marunouchi is that you're right next to some of the city's most famous luxury shops, so you can take a break from walking to do some window shopping or grab a coffee. If you're up for it, check out one of the

Michelin-starred restaurants in the area, though prices will be steep—expect to pay **¥10,000 and up** for a high-end meal.

When it comes to **New Year's traditions**, you'll find people flocking to **Meiji Shrine** for **hatsumode**, which is the first shrine visit of the year. This is one of the busiest spots for New Year's Eve, and it's located right next to **Harajuku Station**, easily accessible by the **JR Yamanote Line**. People line up here to pray for good fortune for the coming year, and the atmosphere is a mix of excitement and reflection. You'll also find food stalls set up outside the shrine selling **takoyaki**, **yakitori**, and **taiyaki**—all for around **¥500 to ¥700** each. The shrine itself has a deep history, dedicated to **Emperor Meiji** and **Empress Shoken**, and it's one of the most significant spiritual sites in the city. If you're up for it, stick around for the **Joya no Kane** ceremony at **Zojo-ji Temple**, where the temple bell rings **108 times** to cleanse you of the previous year's sins. Zojo-ji is located near **Hamamatsucho Station** on the **JR Yamanote Line**, and it's worth the trip for the peaceful vibe.

Winter here also means **fewer tourists**, and you'll definitely notice that the usually packed spots like **Senso-ji Temple** in **Asakusa** feel a lot more relaxed. You won't have to deal with long lines or crowds, which makes it the perfect time to explore the main attractions without feeling rushed. Getting to **Senso-ji** is easy—just take the **Tokyo Metro Ginza Line** to **Asakusa Station**, and you're practically right there. After visiting the temple, walk around the **Nakamise Shopping Street**, where you can pick up traditional souvenirs and try some **street food** like **ningyo-yaki** (small cakes filled with red bean paste) for about **¥300 to ¥500**.

For packing, don't underestimate the **cold**, especially in the evenings. The temperature stays around **5°C to 10°C**, but with the wind, it can feel much colder. You'll want to bring a **warm coat, scarf, gloves**, and definitely something to cover your ears if you're planning to be outside for the illuminations or New Year's events. You don't need snow boots, but **comfortable walking shoes** are a must since you'll be on your feet a lot. If you're sensitive to the cold, layering is key—wearing a few lighter layers under your coat will help you adjust when you're moving between the cold outdoors and heated stores or cafes.

NARITA AIRPORT TO CENTRAL TOKYO

When you arrive at **Narita Airport**, getting into the city quickly is important, and how you get there depends on where you're staying, your budget, and how much time you want to spend on the road.

If speed matters most to you, the **Keisei Skyliner** is by far the fastest. It'll take you directly to **Ueno Station** in **41 minutes**, costing around **¥2,500**. **Ueno** is a great spot for transfers, as it connects you to the **JR Yamanote Line**, which circles the main districts like **Shibuya, Shinjuku**, and **Tokyo Station**. Skyliner trains leave every **20 to 40 minutes**, so you won't be hanging around long, and the best part? You get a **reserved seat**, which makes it more relaxing after a long flight. Once at Ueno, you can visit **Ueno Park**, the **Tokyo National Museum**, or wander over to the **Ameya-Yokocho Market** for some street food, like **yakitori** or **takoyaki**. If you're heading to areas nearby like **Asakusa**, you can easily grab a short **taxi ride** or hop on the **Tokyo Metro Ginza Line** from Ueno.

If you're headed to **Shinjuku, Shibuya**, or **Tokyo Station**, the JR **Narita Express (N'EX)** is a direct option. It's slightly slower than the Skyliner—taking **53 minutes** to **Tokyo Station**—but it's super convenient if your hotel or Airbnb is near **Shinjuku** (about **80 minutes**) or **Shibuya** (around **70 minutes**). The fare is **¥3,070** one-way, and you'll enjoy **reserved seating** and **luggage storage**, which is helpful if you've got a lot of bags. The **Narita Express** runs every **30 to 60 minutes** and connects to some of the busiest, most famous areas of the city. Once you're at **Shibuya Station**, you can step out and see the iconic **Shibuya Crossing**, visit the **Hachiko Statue**, or explore **Shibuya's shopping and dining scene**.

If convenience matters more than speed, especially if you're staying at a big hotel, the **Airport Limousine Bus** is your best bet. It takes around **80 to 100 minutes**, depending on traffic, but it drops you off directly at major hotels in areas like **Shinjuku, Roppongi**, or **Ikebukuro**, so you won't have to worry about dragging your luggage through train stations or making any transfers. The cost is about **¥3,200**, and the buses leave regularly from **Terminal 1** and **Terminal 2/3**. If you're staying in **Roppongi**, you'll be surrounded by a mix of nightlife, fancy restaurants, and cultural spots like the **Mori Art Museum** and **Roppongi Hills**, making it a lively place to explore as soon as you settle in.

For who want to save money, the **Keisei Limited Express** is your budget-friendly option. It's not as fast, taking about **75 minutes** to **Ueno**, but the fare is only **¥1,000**. While there's no reserved seating or luggage storage, it's perfect if you're not in a rush and want to save some cash. Once you reach Ueno, you can easily explore the area or hop on the **Yamanote Line** to get to your final destination.

Depending on where you need to go and how quickly you want to get there, each of these options has its advantages. The **Keisei Skyliner** is quick and efficient for reaching **Ueno**, while the **Narita Express** offers direct service to key districts like **Shinjuku** and **Shibuya**. If you prefer convenience, the **Airport**

Limousine Bus will take you straight to your hotel, and for those traveling on a budget, the **Keisei Limited Express** is a solid, affordable choice.

HANEDA AIRPORT TO CENTRAL TOKYO

When you land at **Haneda Airport**, located in **Ota Ward** about **14 kilometers** from central Tokyo, you've got a few solid options to get into the city, depending on your budget and how quickly you want to arrive. The three main choices are the **Keikyu Line, Tokyo Monorail**, and **taxis**.

If you're looking for the **fastest and cheapest option**, the **Keikyu Line** is your best bet. You'll get from **Haneda Airport Terminal 3** to **Shinagawa Station** in about **13 minutes**, with trains leaving every **10 to 15 minutes**. The ticket costs around **¥300**, which is great for a quick ride. Once you arrive at **Shinagawa Station**, you'll be in a major hub with easy connections to the **JR Yamanote Line**, which can take you to key spots like **Shibuya, Shinjuku**, and **Tokyo Station**. **Shinagawa** itself is a busy business district with a lot of hotels, restaurants, and direct access to other train lines if you need to continue on. The area around **Shinagawa Station** has plenty of places to eat, ranging from quick bites like **ramen** to more upscale sushi options, so you'll have no problem finding a meal before heading out to explore.

If you prefer a **scenic route** with a bit more comfort, the **Tokyo Monorail** is another good choice. The monorail connects **Haneda Airport** to **Hamamatsucho Station** in about **18 minutes**, and the ticket costs **¥500**. The ride takes you along Tokyo Bay, offering great views of the city as you get closer. **Hamamatsucho Station** is close to famous landmarks like **Tokyo Tower** and **Zojo-ji Temple**, which are only about a **10-minute walk** from the station. If you want to explore these spots before heading to your hotel, it's a convenient place to start. From **Hamamatsucho**, you can also transfer easily to the **JR Yamanote Line**, which loops around all of Tokyo's major neighborhoods. The trains leave every **3 to 5 minutes**, so it's quick and efficient.

Now, if you've got **heavy luggage** or just want to avoid the hassle of public transport, a **taxi** might be your best option. Taxis are right outside **Terminal 3**, and the ride into central areas like **Shibuya, Shinjuku**, or **Tokyo Station** takes around **30 to 40 minutes**, depending on traffic. The cost for a taxi ride is typically between **¥6,000 and ¥8,000**, but it's worth it if you're looking for a **door-to-door service** with no need to deal with transfers or stations. You'll be dropped off directly at your hotel, which is a major convenience if you're arriving late or just don't want to deal with crowded trains after a long flight. If you're heading to **Shibuya**, you'll find yourself right in the middle of one of Tokyo's liveliest areas, filled with shopping, nightlife, and iconic spots like **Shibuya Crossing** and the **Hachiko Statue.**

Each option gives you a slightly different experience, but all of them will get you into the city easily. The **Keikyu Line** is fast, cheap, and efficient if you're heading to **Shinagawa** and need to connect to other lines. The **Tokyo Monorail** offers a comfortable and scenic ride to **Hamamatsucho**, perfect if you want to start your trip with a great view of the city. And if you want the most convenient option, especially with a lot of luggage, a **taxi** will get you to your destination directly without the need for transfers.

CHOOSING THE PERFECT PLACE

LUXURY TRAVELERS: WHERE TO STAY

Ginza, **Roppongi**, and **Shibuya** offer the perfect blend of upscale accommodations, world-class dining, and shopping. Each neighborhood has its own unique vibe, but all three provide the high-end touches you're after, whether it's elegant hotels, fine dining, or exclusive boutiques. Let's break down what you can expect in each of these areas, along with all the important details you need to know to make your stay perfect.

Ginza is Tokyo's most upscale district and one of the most luxurious neighborhoods in the world. You'll find it located in **Chuo Ward**, easily accessible by the **Tokyo Metro Ginza Line** (get off at **Ginza Station**) or the **JR Yamanote Line** (get off at **Yurakucho Station**). Here, you can book a stay at the **Mandarin Oriental**, **Peninsula Tokyo**, or **Conrad Tokyo**, all offering stunning views of the city and top-tier services. Staying in **Ginza** means you're right in the heart of the city's luxury shopping, with iconic streets like **Chuo-dori** and **Harumi-dori** lined with designer stores such as **Chanel**, **Louis Vuitton**, and **Gucci**. You'll be just a short walk from the famous **Mitsukoshi Department Store**, where the **depachika** (food basement) is a must-visit for picking up gourmet snacks and gifts, with perfectly packaged sweets and high-end bento boxes available for around **¥1,500 to ¥3,000.**

Ginza isn't just about shopping—its dining scene is world-renowned. For an unforgettable sushi experience, head to **Sukiyabashi Jiro** (make sure to reserve well in advance), or try **Ginza Kojyu** for **kaiseki** dining that celebrates seasonal ingredients. Meals here can cost from **¥20,000 to ¥30,000**, but they are worth every yen for the quality and the service. After dinner, head up to one of the many rooftop bars in the area, like the **Conrad's TwentyEight Bar & Lounge**, where you can sip on cocktails while overlooking the bright city lights. **Ginza** is also home to plenty of cultural spots like the **Kabukiza Theatre**, where you can catch a traditional **kabuki** performance, blending perfectly with the district's modern luxury. Getting around is easy, and you'll find taxis readily available in this area, making your stay as smooth as possible.

Now, if you want something more modern but with a lively cultural twist, **Roppongi** is the place to be. Situated in **Minato Ward**, you can easily get here by the **Tokyo Metro Hibiya Line** or the **Toei Oedo Line** (get off at **Roppongi Station**). The **Ritz-Carlton Tokyo**, located in the **Midtown Tower**, and the **Grand Hyatt Tokyo**, located within **Roppongi Hills**, are top choices for luxury stays, both offering stunning views of **Tokyo Tower** and, on clear days, **Mount Fuji**. Staying in **Roppongi** also puts you close to some of the city's best cultural experiences. You'll be just steps from the **Mori Art Museum**, located at the top of **Roppongi Hills**, where you can enjoy contemporary art exhibitions with a view of the skyline. The **Tokyo Midtown Complex** houses luxury brands like **Issey Miyake** and **Dunhill**, as well as an excellent selection of fine dining options. You can try **Ukai-tei** for an incredible **teppanyaki** meal, where dinner will typically cost around **¥20,000 to ¥25,000** per person. After dinner, stroll around the **Midtown Garden**, a peaceful urban oasis, or catch a late-night cocktail at the **Ritz-Carlton's** bar on the **45th floor**, which boasts one of the best views in the city.

Roppongi is also known for its nightlife, offering a mix of high-end bars and nightclubs if you want to see the city come alive after dark. Don't miss the chance to visit **Roppongi Hills' Sky Deck**, an open-air observation deck, for a 360-degree view of the city, with tickets costing **¥2,000** for access. With **Roppongi's** central location, getting around is easy with frequent buses and taxis, but it's also a very walkable area, with plenty to see right around your hotel.

If you want a vibrant area with a trendy vibe while still enjoying luxury, **Shibuya** is another great option. The **Cerulean Tower Tokyu Hotel** and **Trunk Hotel** offer high-end stays in the heart of one of Tokyo's most iconic districts. **Shibuya** is famous for its buzzing atmosphere and the **Shibuya Crossing**, but you can also find quieter, more upscale experiences just a short walk away in **Aoyama**. To get to **Shibuya**, use the **JR Yamanote Line** (get off at **Shibuya Station**), which makes it a very convenient area for transport. If you're staying in **Cerulean Tower**, you'll have access to large, modern rooms with incredible city views and a range of fine dining restaurants right in the hotel.

Around **Shibuya**, you'll find plenty of stylish cafes and high-end dining options hidden among the busy streets. Head to **Kaikaya by the Sea** for a fusion of Japanese and Western seafood, with meals ranging from **¥4,000 to ¥8,000**, or try **Cé La Vi Tokyo,** a rooftop bar and restaurant that offers excellent cocktails and a stunning view of the city for around **¥1,500 to ¥2,000** per drink. If you feel like exploring further, **Aoyama** is only a **10-minute walk** from **Shibuya Crossing,** and offers more designer shops and exclusive cafes, perfect for a quiet afternoon of shopping.

BUDGET-FRIENDLY: HOSTELS AND CAPSULE HOTELS

Asakusa and **Ueno** are exactly where you want to be. Both areas are packed with affordable accommodation, rich culture, and easy access to public transport, making them ideal if you want to save on your stay without missing out on the city's best experiences. Let's dive into the details so you know exactly what to expect, how to get there, and what's around.

Asakusa is an old, traditional neighborhood located in **Taito Ward,** well-known for its iconic **Senso-ji Temple.** When you stay in this area, you're step-ping into one of the city's most culturally rich districts. Hostels and capsule hotels here offer excellent value. One of the top picks is **Khaosan Tokyo Origami,** located on **2-6-7 Asakusa.** This hostel is just a **5-minute walk** from **Asakusa Station,** making it super convenient for getting around. The **Ginza Line** will take you directly to major areas like **Shibuya** and **Ginza,** and the station also connects you to the **Asakusa Line,** perfect if you're coming from **Haneda** or **Narita Airport.** Prices at **Khaosan Tokyo Origami** range from **¥2,500 to ¥3,500 per night** for shared dorms. This hostel is clean, comfortable, and very social, so it's a great place to meet fellow travelers. You've also got access to a shared kitchen, which means you can prepare your meals and save even more on food.

In **Asakusa**, you're just minutes from some of the best street food stalls, especially along **Nakamise Shopping Street**, right next to **Senso-ji Temple**. For a cheap and tasty meal, grab a serving of **taiyaki** (fish-shaped cakes filled with sweet red bean paste) for around ¥300, or **tempura** from local spots near **Kaminarimon Gate** for under ¥1,000. Plus, **Senso-ji Temple** is a must-visit, offering a glimpse into Tokyo's history and tradition. It's free to enter, and wandering through the temple grounds during the day or at night when it's beautifully illuminated is an experience you can't miss.

Another affordable option in **Asakusa** is the **Nine Hours Asakusa Capsule Hotel**, located on **2-6-15 Asakusa**. If you're up for a more futuristic experience, this place is perfect. Capsules are sleek, clean, and surprisingly comfortable, offering you a personal space that's compact yet practical. Prices range from ¥3,000 to ¥4,000 per night, depending on the season. It's located just a **2-minute walk from Asakusa Station**, so again, you're well-connected. Nearby, you've got access to the **Sumida River**, where you can take relaxing riverside walks or hop on a **water bus** to other parts of the city.

Now, over in **Ueno**, another fantastic spot for budget travelers, you'll find just as many affordable stays but with a slightly different vibe. **Ueno**, also in **Taito Ward**, is famous for its large park, **Ueno Park**, home to several museums like the **Tokyo National Museum** and **Ueno Zoo**. Staying at **Sakura Hostel Ueno**, located on **2-6-11 Iriya, Taito-ku**, puts you right in the middle of all the action. It's a **10-minute walk from Ueno Station**, which connects you to the JR **Yamanote Line**, one of the most important lines in the city that loops around all the major areas. Dorms here range from ¥2,500 to ¥3,500 per night, and the hostel is well-equipped with a shared kitchen, lounge, and free Wi-Fi.

What's fantastic about **Ueno** is its proximity to **Ameya-Yokocho Market**, a bustling shopping street where you can find everything from clothes to electronics, but more importantly, **cheap eats**. You can grab **yakitori** (grilled chicken skewers) for around ¥200 a stick, or enjoy a filling bowl of **ramen** for under ¥800 at one of the many small ramen shops. **Ueno Park** is free to explore and offers a peaceful escape from the busy city streets, especially during **cherry blossom season** in the spring. Plus, many of the museums in the park, like the **Tokyo National Museum**, have affordable entrance fees (around ¥600 to ¥1,000 depending on the exhibit), so you can spend a day soaking up the culture without spending too much.

If you're after a capsule hotel experience in **Ueno**, look no further than **Capsule Net Omotenashi no Oyado**, located at **6-8-20 Ueno**. This capsule hotel is perfect for those who want to unwind after a long day of sightseeing, offering an onsen-style bath and sauna. Prices range from **¥3,000 to ¥4,000 per night**, and it's located **5 minutes from Ueno Station**, making it easy to get around the city. The capsules are clean and comfortable, with personal lighting, outlets for your devices, and shared bathroom facilities that are well-maintained.

FAMILY-FRIENDLY STAYS

These areas not only have **larger hotel rooms** and **great family-friendly amenities**, but they are also **packed with attractions that both kids and adults can enjoy**, and are **conveniently located near transport options**, making your trip easier.

Odaiba is a **family-friendly man-made island** in **Tokyo Bay**, known for its **open spaces** and **modern attractions**. It's the ideal area for families who need some room to breathe and want easy access to **waterfront parks** and **entertainment**. You can easily reach Odaiba using the **Yurikamome Line**, which is a fun, elevated monorail ride that crosses over the **Rainbow Bridge** and offers great views of the city. The **Yurikamome Line** runs frequently, and you can catch it from **Shimbashi Station**, with a short ride to **Daiba Station** (about 15 minutes). Once there, everything is within walking distance, including your hotel, restaurants, and attractions.

A fantastic family-friendly hotel in Odaiba is the **Hilton Tokyo Odaiba**, located at **1-9-1 Daiba**. This hotel is popular among families for its **spacious rooms** that offer stunning views of **Tokyo Bay** and the **Rainbow Bridge**. The family rooms here are larger than average Tokyo rooms, and they even offer extra beds and cribs for families with young children. Rates typically start from **¥25,000 per night** for a family room, depending on the season. Plus, the hotel features several restaurants catering to families, so you can find everything from Japanese cuisine to Western-style options without leaving the hotel.

Right next to the hotel, you'll find **Aqua City Odaiba**, a large shopping complex filled with family dining options, including **Gundam Café** (a hit with kids who love robots) and **Burger King**, for a quick, affordable meal. Attractions in Odaiba include **Legoland Discovery Center**, which is **a 5-minute walk** from **Daiba Station**, and **Tokyo Joypolis**, an indoor amusement park packed with arcade games and virtual reality rides. Admission to **Legoland Discovery Center** costs about **¥2,400** for children and **¥2,800** for adults, and Tokyo Joypolis is priced at around **¥4,500** for a day pass.

When you're ready for some fresh air, **Odaiba Seaside Park** offers a peaceful, open space where the kids can run around or play on the beach, and it's free. You can also visit the **Miraikan**, or **National Museum of Emerging Science and Innovation**, where the kids will love interacting with robots and other hands-on exhibits. Entry costs around **¥620 for adults** and **¥210 for children**. Miraikan is about a **10-minute walk** from **Daiba Station**.

Moving on to **Ikebukuro**, this bustling district in **Toshima Ward** is packed with **family-friendly attractions** that make it another excellent choice for families. You can easily get to **Ikebukuro** via the **JR Yamanote Line** to **Ikebukuro Station**, which is a major transportation hub. The area is home to **Sunshine City**, a large shopping and entertainment complex that includes an **aquarium, planetarium**, and the popular **Pokemon Center Mega Tokyo**.

One of the best family hotels in Ikebukuro is **Hotel Metropolitan Tokyo Ikebukuro**, located at **1-6-1 Nishi-Ikebukuro**, just **2 minutes from Ikebukuro Station**. Rooms here are designed for families, offering **larger spaces** and amenities like **extra beds and cribs**. Prices start around **¥20,000 per night** for a family room, depending on the season. The hotel is also close to **Minami-Ikebukuro Park**, a green space where kids can play while you relax, and it's just a **5-minute walk** from the hotel.

If your kids love Pokémon, they'll go crazy at the **Pokemon Center Mega Tokyo**, located in **Sunshine City**. This mega-store sells everything Pokémon, and it's a must-visit for fans. **Namjatown**, also inside **Sunshine City**, offers quirky attractions and themed food, which is sure to keep the kids entertained for hours. Tickets for **Namjatown** are **¥500 for entry**, with additional costs for attractions inside. Right next door is **Sunshine Aquarium**, where you can see everything from jellyfish to penguins, with tickets priced around **¥2,400 for adults** and **¥1,200 for children**.

For eating out in Ikebukuro, **Sunshine City** is full of family-friendly restaurants. You can grab a casual bite at **Pepper Lunch** for around **¥1,000 per person**, or enjoy sushi at **Sushiro** in the same building. Everything is close, making it easy to manage with kids, and you won't have to travel far to find good food and entertainment.

PRE-TRIP CHECKLIST

Before you get ready to fly, there are several critical things to lock down to ensure a smooth, hassle-free trip. Let's break it down with all the **details you need** to prepare efficiently, covering everything from paperwork to practical tips.

Japan doesn't mess around with these rules, and you could get denied entry if your passport is expiring soon. If your passport is close to expiring, renew it now —it could take a few weeks. Also, make **photocopies**. One for your luggage, one for a trusted person at home, and maybe even a photo of it saved securely online. Better safe than sorry.

Next, **check the visa requirements for your country**. Most people from countries like the **United States, Canada, UK, Australia, and European Union** don't need a visa if they're staying for less than **90 days**—you'll get a tourist stamp upon arrival. However, if you're from a country that requires a visa, head to the **Japanese Embassy website** or consulate in your area. The process can take time, so don't wait until the last minute. Make sure all your documents, such as proof of accommodation and return tickets, are in order before applying.

Travel insurance is non-negotiable. While Japan is incredibly safe, unexpected things can happen, and you don't want to be unprepared if they do. Healthcare in Japan is world-class, but it can get expensive for tourists. Make sure your insurance covers **medical emergencies, cancellations, and any unforeseen disruptions**. You'll also want to include **coverage for natural disasters**, as Japan is known for its earthquakes. Some policies even include trip interruption due to weather, and you'll be thankful if you need to use it. Check if your credit card offers automatic travel insurance when booking flights—some do, but make sure it's robust enough.

If you plan on visiting beyond Tokyo, you'll want to buy a **Japan Rail Pass (JR Pass)** before leaving your country. This pass is a great deal if you're planning to travel to places like **Kyoto, Osaka, or Hiroshima**. It gives you **unlimited rides on JR trains** for a set number of days (7, 14, or 21), but the key is that you **have to buy it before you get to Japan**. It's not sold in Japan itself. You'll receive an exchange voucher in the mail, which you'll swap for the actual pass once you arrive—usually at a JR office in the airport or main train stations. The price starts at around ¥29,650 **for a 7-day pass**, but the savings add up quickly if you're taking multiple long-distance trains. Pro tip: **exchange your voucher at the JR East Travel Service Center in Narita or Haneda Airport** if you plan on using the Shinkansen (bullet trains) shortly after landing.

For getting around Tokyo, **Suica** or **Pasmo** cards are absolute must-haves. These prepaid IC cards are **rechargeable** and work on **trains, buses, and even in convenience stores**. You can purchase them from ticket machines at **Narita or Haneda Airport** as soon as you arrive. They're also available at most **JR stations**. They'll save you from having to buy tickets every time you board a train, and you can top them up easily at kiosks in any station. These cards also work for purchases at places like **7-Eleven, Lawson**, and even **vending machines** across the city, making them extremely convenient. Expect to load ¥2,000–¥3,000 at the start (around ¥500 **is a deposit**, and the rest is for travel).

Before you go, check out the **vaccination recommendations**. Japan doesn't have any mandatory vaccines for travelers, but it's always smart to ensure you're up-to-date on basic shots like **tetanus, diphtheria, polio, and hepatitis A**. Depending on when you're traveling, especially if it's during the colder months (December–February), getting a **flu shot** might be a good idea, too. Though Japan has high hygiene standards, it's always best to be prepared.

Now, if there are particular **experiences or attractions** that are high on your must-do list, especially those that tend to get crowded, like the **Ghibli Museum** in **Mitaka** (about 20 minutes from **Shinjuku Station** on the **JR Chuo Line**), it's essential to **book tickets in advance**. The Ghibli Museum, for example, releases tickets exactly **three months in advance**, and they sell out within hours. Same goes for themed cafes, like the **Pokemon Café in Nihonbashi** or the **Robot Restaurant in Shinjuku**—you'll want to reserve seats ahead of time.

For visiting **Tokyo Skytree** (in **Sumida**), it's smart to book tickets online beforehand to avoid long lines. This can save you a lot of time, especially if you're going during peak travel times. A **general admission ticket** for the **350-meter observation deck** starts around **¥2,100**, and you can also opt for **fast-track tickets** to skip the wait.

Lastly, **book the airport transfers** in advance. If you're landing at **Narita Airport**, the **Keisei Skyliner** is the quickest way into **central Tokyo**, taking about **40 minutes** and costing around **¥2,470** to reach **Ueno Station**. If you're arriving at **Haneda**, the **Tokyo Monorail** is a convenient option, reaching **Hamamatsucho Station** in about **13 minutes** for **¥500**. For those preferring door-to-door service, book a **Limousine Bus** or a **private taxi transfer** online ahead of time, especially if you're arriving late at night or with kids.

CHAPTER 3
PUBLIC TRANSPORT

TOKYO'S RAIL NETWORKS: JR, METRO, AND MORE

When you're navigating the city, the **JR Yamanote Line**, the **Tokyo Metro**, and the **Toei Subway** are going to be your main ways to get around.

The **JR Yamanote Line** is the most important, a circular line that loops around central Tokyo and connects the big districts like **Shibuya, Shinjuku, Akihabara, Ueno,** and **Tokyo Station**. This green line is your best friend, running about every **2-3 minutes** from early morning until nearly **midnight**, so you're never waiting long. If you're staying in popular areas like **Shibuya, Shinjuku,** or even near **Tokyo Station**, you'll be using this line a lot because it hits all the major stops without transfers. The best part? If you miss your stop, no stress, just stay on and it'll loop back around—it's basically a **giant circle**.

For places not directly on the Yamanote, the **Tokyo Metro** fills the gaps. The **Ginza Line** (yellow) takes you to famous spots like **Shibuya** or **Asakusa**, which is where you'll want to go for **Senso-ji Temple** and traditional vibes. The **Hibiya Line** (gray) runs through **Roppongi**—a nightlife hotspot—and to **Tsukiji** for the fresh seafood markets. This subway system is a bit more extensive, with **nine lines** in total, each with its own color and number system. The **Tokyo Metro** generally runs from **5 AM to around midnight**, and trains come every **3-5 minutes**, so you won't be standing around too long.

Then there's the **Toei Subway**, run by the Tokyo Metropolitan Government. It's not as big as the Metro, but the **Oedo Line** (pink) is vital for reaching neighborhoods like **Shinjuku, Akasaka,** and **Roppongi**. If you're visiting **Roppongi Hills** or **Tokyo Midtown** for art and shopping, this line's loop around the city makes it easy to access these spots. The **Toei lines** have fewer trains than the **Metro**, but they are still quick, coming about every **4-6 minutes**. **Station signs** and **maps** are color-coded and numbered, so once you know your line and destination, just follow the numbers to your platform.

Now, **finding your way inside stations**—especially the giant ones like **Shinjuku** or **Tokyo Station**—can be tricky. These stations are practically cities themselves, with tons of exits, so always know your **exit number** in advance. Each exit leads to a different part of the area, and walking from one exit to another inside the station can take up to **10-15 minutes**. For example, **Shinjuku Station** has more than **200 exits**, so make sure you know which one you need. Once you're out of the station, you'll be in a district full of restaurants, shopping, and cafes—take your time to explore.

To make your trip easier, definitely download **Google Maps** or **Navitime**. These apps will give you **real-time directions**, show you which platform to head for, how much the fare will be, and even when the next train leaves. They'll also tell you which exit to take—saving you from the headache of getting lost inside giant stations. And if you're wondering about transfers between different systems, don't worry—the **Yamanote Line, Metro,** and **Toei Subway** are all interconnected. You might have to exit through a gate and tap your **Suica** or **Pasmo** card when switching systems, but everything is designed to make it smooth.

If you're near a station like **Shibuya** or **Ueno**, you'll find tons of food spots around the exits. At **Shibuya Station**, for instance, just step out of the **Hachiko Exit** and you're in the middle of **Shibuya Crossing**, surrounded by **ramen shops, sushi spots**, and even **trendy cafes**. In **Ueno**, you're right next to **Ameyoko Market**, famous for cheap eats like **yakitori** (grilled chicken skewers) and **takoyaki** (octopus balls) with prices starting around **¥300**.

Lastly, to avoid getting confused about the trains and stations, always check the **station maps**—these are everywhere, even in English—and you'll quickly get the hang of how the **color-coded lines** and **station numbers** work together. For example, you'll see **G-01** for the **Ginza Line**, which tells you where you are and helps you figure out which direction you're heading. Follow the signs and you'll be hopping around the city like a pro.

SUICA, PASMO, AND THE JR PASS: WHICH CARD IS RIGHT FOR YOU?

If you're mainly exploring **Tokyo** or doing a few short trips nearby, **Suica** or **Pasmo** will be your best friends, and these cards can be used on all trains, buses, and even at convenience stores. But, if you're planning to travel further, like heading to places like **Kyoto, Osaka**, or **Hiroshima**, the **JR Pass** is going to save you money and make your travel much smoother.

First, let's dive into **Suica** and **Pasmo**. These **IC cards** are super handy for getting around **Tokyo**. You can use them for **JR East trains, Tokyo Metro, buses**, and even at some **vending machines** and **convenience stores** like **Lawson, FamilyMart**, and **7-Eleven**. You can pick up a **Suica card** at any **JR East station**, including **Shibuya, Shinjuku**, or **Tokyo Station**. If you're flying into **Narita Airport** or **Haneda Airport**, you can easily get a **Suica** or **Pasmo** card there too. **Pasmo** works exactly the same, but you'll find it at **Tokyo Metro stations**. Once you have your card, it comes pre-loaded with **¥1,500**, plus a **¥500 deposit**, so you're ready to start traveling immediately. You can charge the card at any train station or convenience store—just look for the machines that say "**Charge**," and you can top it up with **¥1,000, ¥2,000**, or more.

What makes these cards really cool is that they work almost everywhere in Japan. Let's say you're spending a few days in **Kyoto** or **Osaka**; your **Suica** or **Pasmo** card will still work there for most public transportation, so you don't have to buy separate tickets. This is really helpful when you're bouncing between cities. And if you find yourself with extra money on the card at the end of your trip, you can return it at any major **JR East** or **Metro station** and get your **deposit** back, along with whatever balance is left.

Now, when it comes to **traveling outside of Tokyo**—especially if you're visiting **Kyoto, Osaka, Hiroshima**, or even further like **Hokkaido**—that's when the **JR Pass** comes in. The **JR Pass** is designed for tourists who want to explore multiple cities. You'll need to **buy it before arriving in Japan**, and you can exchange your voucher for the pass at a **JR Exchange Office** when you land, either at **Narita** or **Haneda Airports**, or at big stations like **Tokyo Station** or **Shinjuku**.

The **JR Pass** allows for **unlimited travel** on all **JR trains**, including shinkansen (bullet trains), except for the **Nozomi** and **Mizuho** services. That means if you're planning to visit places like **Kyoto, Osaka**, or **Nagano**, this pass will save you a lot of money. A **7-day JR Pass** costs about ¥29,650, which might seem like a lot upfront, but a round trip between **Tokyo and Kyoto** can already cost around ¥28,000, so the pass practically pays for itself with just one trip. Plus, you can also use the pass for local JR lines within Tokyo, so it's super versatile. To use it, just show your pass at the **manned gates** (don't try to use it at the automatic gates) and you're good to go.

One of the great things about the **JR Pass** is that it's not just for shinkansen. You can also use it on JR buses and JR ferries, like the one to **Miyajima Island** near **Hiroshima**, which makes it even more valuable. And if you want to reserve a seat on the shinkansen, just head to the **JR ticket office** (called **Midori no Madoguchi**) at any JR station, show them your pass, and they'll book you a seat at no extra charge.

So, if you're spending most of your time in **Tokyo** or the surrounding areas, **Suica** or **Pasmo** will handle almost everything. You can ride the **JR Yamanote Line**, the **Tokyo Metro**, and buses around the city. But if you're planning on going further out—say a few trips to **Kyoto, Osaka**, or **Nikko**—then the **JR Pass** will definitely be worth it.

Here's a practical tip: If you're staying near popular spots like **Shibuya, Shinjuku**, or **Ginza**, grab a **Suica** or **Pasmo**. You'll be able to hop on the **Tokyo Metro**, **JR Yamanote Line**, or buses with ease, and you can also use the card for small purchases like a snack at **FamilyMart** or a bottle of water at a vending machine. If you're going to places further like **Kyoto** or **Osaka**, then the **JR Pass** is what you need, and it'll let you use shinkansen and other JR lines without buying separate tickets every time.

Suica and **Pasmo** are your easy, everyday cards for Tokyo and short trips, while the **JR Pass** is your best bet for traveling across Japan.

STEP-BY-STEP GUIDE TO NAVIGATING TRAINS AND BUSES

Let's start with the trains. If you're not using a **Suica** or **Pasmo** card (which is the easiest way to travel), you'll need to buy a ticket at the **ticket machines**. The machines are located right at the entrance of every train station, and there's usually a big **fare map** above them showing the price to every station. For example, if you're at **Shinjuku Station** and heading to **Ueno**, the map will show that it costs **around ¥200**. You simply enter that amount on the machine, pay, and grab your ticket. **Shinjuku Station** is located on **Yasukuni Street**, and it connects you to a variety of neighborhoods, so make sure to look at the station map for the correct exit.

Now, if you've got a **Suica** or **Pasmo** card, things get even easier. You can pick up these cards from ticket machines or counters at major stations like **Tokyo Station, Shibuya Station**, or even directly at the airport (both **Narita** and **Haneda**). They cost **around ¥2,000**, including **¥500** deposit, and you can top them up as needed. To use these cards, all you do is **tap them at the entrance gates**—it automatically deducts the fare based on how far you travel. If you're at a major station like **Shibuya**, which is on **Inokashira Street**, just tap in and follow the signs for your platform.

Once inside, stations are laid out with clear signs in both **Japanese** and **English**. Train lines are color-coded, so if you're taking the **Yamanote Line**, look for green, and if you're using the **Tokyo Metro Ginza Line**, follow the yellow signs. The key is knowing your platform number and **which direction you're heading**. Let's say you're going from **Shibuya** to **Harajuku**—the signs will direct you to the correct side of the platform. **Harajuku Station**, for example, is just one stop away and takes only a few minutes.

Buses, on the other hand, are a bit different. When you hop on a bus in **Tokyo**, you usually get in from the **middle door**. You won't pay immediately. Find a seat, and when you're approaching your stop, press the **stop button**. When you leave, you'll either tap your **Suica** or **Pasmo** card at the front of the bus, or if you're paying with cash, it's **around ¥210** for a typical city ride. One of the most useful routes is the bus that runs from **Asakusa** to **Ueno**, especially if you're heading to **Ueno Park** or visiting the **Tokyo National Museum**.

As you may know already the app **Google Maps** or **Navitime** will be your best friends when figuring out bus routes, especially since **some bus stops** may not have English signs. They'll tell you exactly which bus to take, where the stop is, and even the best times to catch it. For example, if you're leaving from **Ueno Station** and heading to **Asakusa**, Google Maps will guide you on exactly which bus stop to find, and whether there's any delay.

If you're using both **JR** trains and the **Tokyo Metro**, keep in mind that they are separate networks, but they're well-connected. The **Yamanote Line** (JR) runs in a loop around central Tokyo and hits all the major spots—**Shibuya, Shinjuku, Akihabara**, and **Tokyo Station**. But when you need to head deeper into specific districts like **Ginza** or **Asakusa**, the **Tokyo Metro** or **Toei Subway** lines are usually your best bet.

Now, you might want to eat something while you're out and about, and most **train stations** have plenty of food options inside. **Shinjuku Station** and **Tokyo Station** are packed with places to grab food. In **Shinjuku Station**, you can find **depachika** (department store basements) full of bento boxes, sushi, and sweets. At **Tokyo Station**, in a place called **Ramen Street**, you can find several top-notch ramen shops. Prices for ramen typically start around **¥900**, and it's worth grabbing a meal here before you continue visiting.

Always check the **exit numbers** to avoid wandering too far from your destination. For example, if you're visiting the **Senso-ji Temple** in **Asakusa**, you'll want to exit at **Exit 1** from **Asakusa Station**. The temple is about a five-minute walk from there.

Always keep an eye out for **station maps**, especially in the larger hubs like

Shibuya or **Shinjuku**. These maps will show you which exit to take, and many also point out nearby attractions, restaurants, and shopping spots.

ROUTES SHINJUKU TO ASAKUSA

Traveling from **Shinjuku to Asakusa**, here's everything you need to know, from the specific stations to what's around when you get there. This route is straightforward and well-connected, and I'll walk you through the details with exact times, locations, and recommendations so you won't miss a thing.

Start at **Shinjuku Station**, located in the heart of one of the busiest districts in the city. If you're not familiar with it, this station can feel like a maze—it has multiple entrances and exits, so be sure to follow the signs carefully to get to the **JR Chuo Line**. This line is your first step. You're looking for the **Rapid (Chuo Line)** that goes towards **Tokyo Station**. The **Rapid trains** usually depart from **Platform 7 or 8** and they will take you to **Kanda Station**. This part of the trip will take about **10 minutes**, and you'll pass several stops along the way, like **Yotsuya** and **Ochanomizu**. The fare for this section is around **¥200-¥220** depending on your route.

Once you arrive at **Kanda Station**, exit the JR platforms and follow the signs for the **Tokyo Metro Ginza Line**. Kanda is a smaller station compared to Shinjuku, so navigating it is easier. The Ginza Line, marked by orange signs, is on a different level. You'll need to follow the stairs or escalators down to the metro line. This is a super convenient subway line that will take you right to **Asakusa**. Board a train heading toward **Asakusa Station**—the ride takes about **15 minutes**, stopping at places like **Ueno** and **Tawaramachi**. You'll arrive at **Asakusa Station** on the Ginza Line, just minutes away from one of the most iconic areas in the city. The fare for this section will cost around **¥200**.

As soon as you step off the train at **Asakusa Station**, you'll notice the change in atmosphere. The station is close to **Senso-ji Temple**, one of the oldest and most significant temples in Japan. From **Exit 1**, you can walk directly to **Kaminarimon Gate**, the grand red gate that marks the entrance to the temple. The walk is only about **5 minutes** from the station, and along the way, you'll pass plenty of street vendors selling snacks like **taiyaki** (fish-shaped cakes filled with sweet red bean paste) and **yakitori** (grilled chicken skewers). You'll want to check out **Nakamise Shopping Street**, where you can find a variety of traditional goods, sweets, and souvenirs. This area buzzes with both tourists and locals alike.

For the best experience, try to visit the temple early in the morning or later in the evening when it's less crowded. If you're into history, you'll appreciate knowing that **Senso-ji** was originally completed in **645 AD**, making it a site with centuries of cultural significance. Don't forget to step into the temple, wash your hands at the **chozuya** (water basin), and make a small offering.

While you're in Asakusa, grab lunch at one of the nearby restaurants. A popular spot is **Daikokuya Tempura**, located at **1-38-10 Asakusa**, where you can try their famous tempura bowl for about **¥2,000**. The tempura here is crisp, light, and a local favorite. Another must-try in Asakusa is **Kagetsudo**, a bakery known for their massive **melonpan** (sweet bread), perfect for a snack while exploring the area. It's located just behind the temple at **2-7-13 Asakusa**, and a melonpan will only set you back around **¥200-¥300**.

Visiting beyond the temple, consider walking along the **Sumida River**, where you can take in views of the **Tokyo Skytree** across the river. There's even a chance to take a **river cruise** from Asakusa, heading to other parts of the city like **Odaiba** or **Hamarikyu Gardens**. The cruises leave from the **Sumida River Pier**, and tickets start at around **¥1,000**, offering a relaxing way to view the city from the water.

For getting back, you can take the same **Ginza Line** from Asakusa Station or explore other routes, such as taking the **Toei Asakusa Line** which connects directly to other parts of the city, including **Nihombashi** or **Haneda Airport** if you're catching a flight. The total round trip will cost you about **¥400-¥500**, making it an affordable and efficient way to explore one of the most famous areas in the city.

With the JR Chuo Line and the Ginza Metro Line, navigating your way between Shinjuku and Asakusa is simple.

BIKING, WALKING, AND DRIVING

BIKING

If you're keen on **biking**, the city has an increasing number of bike-friendly areas, although it's important to know that bike lanes are still not the norm in every part of the city. One of the best services for renting a bike is **Docomo Bike Share**, which allows you to pick up and drop off bikes at multiple docking stations across the city. You'll usually find these stations near **major train stations** in districts like **Shibuya, Shinjuku, Minato**, and **Chiyoda**, and for just **¥150 per 30 minutes**, you get an eco-friendly and active way to explore.

Biking around areas like **Shibuya** or **Roppongi**, you'll experience the energetic buzz of the city but watch out for limited bike lanes on the busier streets like **Meiji-dori** or **Aoyama-dori**. For a more relaxed and scenic ride, **Odaiba** is a great area because of its **wide streets** and **seaside views**. The paths along **Sumida River**, from **Asakusa** toward **Tokyo Skytree**, are also perfect for a laid-back ride with plenty of photo ops along the riverbank. **Yoyogi Park**, located near **Harajuku Station** (right on the **JR Yamanote Line**), is another fantastic spot for biking, with dedicated lanes and a peaceful setting surrounded by trees, a perfect break from the crowded streets.

If you plan to bike around, just make sure to always park in designated bike parking areas, as parking on the sidewalk or in unauthorized areas can lead to fines. These parking spaces are easy to spot around popular spots, and if you're unsure, ask someone for help. Major bike parking areas are found around **Shibuya Station**, **Tokyo Midtown**, and near **Ueno Park**.

FOOT

Walking is one of the best ways to **really get to know the city**, and since **Tokyo** is packed with neighborhoods that beg to be explored on foot, you'll find endless things to see just by strolling around. Start your journey in **Asakusa**, where you can visit the iconic **Senso-ji Temple**, and then wander down **Nakamise-dori**, a bustling street filled with traditional souvenir shops and snacks like **senbei rice crackers** and **taiyaki** (fish-shaped pastries). From there, you can walk along the **Sumida River**, passing peaceful parks and finding great spots to take in the skyline, especially near **Tokyo Skytree**.

Another fantastic walking route takes you through **Harajuku**, starting at **Takeshita Street**, just outside **Harajuku Station** (on the **JR Yamanote Line**). This area is famous for its vibrant fashion culture and quirky shops, and you can easily spend hours browsing or people-watching. From there, head over to **Omotesando**, an elegant tree-lined street that leads to the more sophisticated side of town, filled with high-end stores and cafes.

If you want to escape the modern hustle and bustle, **Yanaka** in **Taito Ward** offers a walk through old **Tokyo**, with its narrow streets, traditional houses, and the charming **Yanaka Ginza** shopping street, where you can find small local food stalls and crafts. This area is easily accessible from **Nippori Station** on the **JR Yamanote Line**, and it feels like stepping back in time.

DRIVING

Driving might not be your first thought when thinking about getting around in **Tokyo**, but it does offer some distinct advantages, especially if you're planning to visit areas outside the city or on the outskirts, like **Hakone** or **Nikko**. Renting a car is simple with rental services like **Toyota Rent-a-Car** offering multiple locations across the city. Expect to pay around **¥7,000 to ¥10,000 per day**, depending on the type of car you rent.

However, driving within the city comes with its own set of challenges. **Traffic can be heavy**, especially during peak hours between **7 AM to 9 AM** and **5 PM to 7 PM**, and parking is not only expensive but also hard to find in busy areas like **Ginza** or **Shibuya**, where rates can go up to **¥800 per hour**. If you're staying in **Shibuya** or **Shinjuku**, you might be better off walking or using public transport. However, **driving out to the countryside**, or even just heading toward the **Tokyo suburbs,** can make renting a car worth it, especially if you want to enjoy the scenic routes around **Mount Fuji** or the **coastal areas**.

Driving rules in Japan can be tricky for foreign travelers, and you'll need to get an **International Driving Permit** before arriving. Also, be prepared for toll roads; many expressways use an **ETC card**, which allows you to drive through toll gates without stopping, and rental agencies typically offer them for an extra fee.

POPULAR BIKING SPOTS

SUMIDA RIVER

One of the most scenic routes you'll find runs along **Sumida River**, stretching from **Sumida Park** near **Asakusa** all the way down to **Tokyo Bay**. **Sumida Park** is easy to reach by getting off at **Asakusa Station** (served by the **Tokyo Metro Ginza Line**, **Toei Asakusa Line**, or the **Tobu Isesaki Line**). As soon as you step out, you'll see many options for renting bikes. One convenient service is **Docomo Bike Share**, where you can rent bikes for around **¥165 per 30 minutes** or opt for a whole day at **¥1,100**.

When you're cycling along the river, you have to stop and admire the view of the iconic **Tokyo Skytree**, which stands proudly above the skyline. It's a popular area tourists during **sakura (cherry blossom) season**, as the entire riverbank is lined with cherry blossom trees. The best time to bike here is in **April**, right when the sakura is in full bloom. Along the way, you can stop by the **Asahi Beer Hall** or pick up a snack at **Nakamise-dori**, a bustling shopping street just outside **Senso-ji Temple**. **Taiyaki** (a fish-shaped pastry filled with sweet red bean) is a local favorite and costs around **¥150**.

There are designated bike parking spots at **Sumida Park** and near **Asakusa**

Station, but you'll need to look out for the signs to avoid parking fines (typically around ¥2,000 if you're in the wrong place).

ODAIBA

If you're looking for a mix of modern architecture and waterfront views, **Odaiba** is the perfect place to explore on two wheels. This futuristic island is accessible via the **Yurikamome Line** to **Daiba Station** or the **Rinkai Line** to **Tokyo Teleport Station**. Once there, you can rent bikes at **Odaiba Seaside Park** for **¥600 for two hours** or **¥1,200 for the day**.

You'll cycle along the wide, flat paths beside **Tokyo Bay**, offering stunning views of **Rainbow Bridge** and the surrounding cityscape. You can start from **Odaiba Beach**, riding towards landmarks like the **Fuji TV Building** and **DiverCity Tokyo Plaza**, home of the life-sized **Gundam Statue**. If you need a break, stop by **Aqua City Odaiba** for lunch or visit the **Odaiba Takoyaki Museum** where you can sample different types of **takoyaki** (octopus-filled dough balls) starting at ¥500.

There are plenty of parking spots near **Aqua City**, **VenusFort**, and the **Odaiba Marine Park**, so it's easy to stop and explore.

YOYOGI PARK

Yoyogi Park is one of the city's largest public parks, perfect for a relaxed bike ride, is located near **Harajuku Station** on the **JR Yamanote Line** and **Meiji-Jingumae Station** on the **Tokyo Metro Chiyoda Line**, this park is famous for its wide open spaces and seasonal beauty, especially during **autumn** when the leaves turn vibrant shades of red and gold.

Bike rentals are available right inside the park for **¥500 per hour**. Yoyogi Park's paths are perfect for families, and after you finish riding, you're just a short walk from **Takeshita Street** in **Harajuku**. This famous street is lined with shops offering quirky fashion and delicious crepes for **¥400-¥500**. If you're more into cultural spots, the **Meiji Shrine** is just next door, and there are bike parking areas near the shrine entrances and **Harajuku Station**.

Where to Rent:

Docomo Bike Share stations are scattered around the city, allowing you to rent and return bikes at different points, making it convenient for those covering more ground. For a day pass, expect to pay around **¥1,100**, and they also offer electric bikes for those who want a smoother ride.

Bike Lanes & Parking:

Tokyo has started to improve its bike lane infrastructure, but it's still important to pay attention to shared paths with pedestrians. You'll find bike lanes in spots like **Sumida River** and **Odaiba**, but always park in designated areas to avoid fines.

WALKING TOURS: SHIBUYA TO OMOTESANDO

You have to start your walking tour at **Shibuya Crossing**, where is located right outside **Shibuya Station** (accessible via JR Yamanote Line, Tokyo Metro Hanzomon Line, and Ginza Line), this iconic intersection is the perfect spot to kick off your adventure. The crossing is at the heart of **Shibuya**, and it's busiest during the day and evening rush hours. To get there, simply exit **Shibuya Station** from the **Hachiko Exit**—you'll know you're in the right place when you see the sea of people moving across the intersection in every direction. It's a spectacle and one of the most photographed places in Tokyo.

Before moving forward, visit the **Hachiko Statue**, located just outside the station near the crossing. The statue honors the loyal dog Hachiko, who famously waited for his owner every day at the station. It's a must-see, and because it's such a popular meeting spot, it's perfect for grabbing a few photos or just taking a quick break before diving into the Shibuya streets.

From here, make your way towards **Center Gai**, a buzzing pedestrian street just across Shibuya Crossing. **Center Gai** is lined with shops, fast food spots, and neon signs overhead. It's a haven for trendy clothing stores, record shops, and entertainment. You'll find both well-known brands and quirky, local fashion. You can easily spend an hour or more browsing the street's offerings. If you're hungry, grab a bite at **Ichiran Ramen** nearby (on **Dogenzaka Street**, about a 5-minute walk from **Center Gai**). A meal here costs about ¥1,000-¥1,200, and you can enjoy a private dining experience with delicious tonkotsu ramen.

Next, head towards **Shibuya 109**, which is located at the top of **Dogenzaka Street**. This multi-level fashion tower is perfect if you want to immerse yourself in the latest Japanese fashion trends. The building houses numerous shops, primarily catering to women, but even if shopping isn't your thing, it's worth taking a look around. It's a hub for the Shibuya youth fashion culture.

After you've soaked up the energy of **Center Gai** and **Shibuya 109**, take a 15-minute walk to **Cat Street**. This quiet, alternative street connects Shibuya to **Omotesando** and is the perfect contrast to the buzz of Shibuya. **Cat Street** offers a more relaxed atmosphere, with indie boutiques, vintage stores, and artisan cafes. You can rent a bike from places like **Hello Cycling** for about **¥200 per 30 minutes**, or just enjoy the walk through this artsy neighborhood. Along the way, stop by **Streamer Coffee Company** on **Cat Street** for some coffee art—this spot is famous for its delicious brews, and a latte will cost around **¥600**.

As you approach **Omotesando**, the vibe shifts towards luxury. You'll see the architecture changing, with sleek, modern buildings lining the streets. **Omotesando Hills** (located on **Omotesando Avenue**) is one of the standout features of this area. Designed by architect **Tadao Ando**, this luxury shopping complex blends high-end fashion stores with art galleries, cafes, and restaurants.

For food in **Omotesando**, try **Maisen Tonkatsu** (located at **4 Chome-8-5 Jingumae, Shibuya City**), famous for its crispy tonkatsu (breaded pork cutlets). The cost for a set meal is typically around **¥1,800-¥2,500**, and it's an ideal spot for lunch after exploring the area.

The walk from **Shibuya Crossing** to **Omotesando** covers about **2 kilometers** and takes **30 to 45 minutes**, depending on how often you stop along the way. You can easily extend your walking tour to **Harajuku** (just a 10-minute walk from **Omotesando**) or explore more of the stylish **Aoyama** area. The best time to take this walk is during the late morning or early afternoon, when the shops are open, and you can enjoy a relaxed pace without too many crowds. Have Fun!

CAR RENTAL INFORMATION

Step 1: What You Need to Rent a Car

The first thing you need to know is that **Japan requires an International Driver's Permit (IDP)** in addition to your regular driver's license. You must get this in your home country before traveling, as you won't be able to rent a car without it, and they cannot be issued in Japan. The IDP is valid for a year, so make sure yours covers the entire period of your stay. Along with this, bring your passport and credit card to the rental office.

Most car rental companies like **Nippon Rent-A-Car**, **Toyota Rent a Car**, and **Times Car Rental** have locations at the main transport hubs. **Haneda Airport** (both **Terminal 1 and 2**) and **Narita Airport** (located at **Terminal 1 and 2**) are popular spots where you can rent cars directly after landing. If you're already in the city, look for branches at **Tokyo Station**, **Shibuya**, or **Shinjuku**, where there are several rental offices within walking distance of the main train exits.

Step 2: Booking and Picking Up the Car

When booking, it's best to reserve online ahead of time. **Prices start around ¥6,000 per day** for a compact car, but if you want something larger like an SUV or a van, expect to pay around **¥10,000 to ¥12,000 per day**. A compact car is typically ideal for driving in urban areas, especially when navigating through **Shibuya** or **Ginza** where streets can be narrow and parking spaces are small.

Once at the rental location, make sure to request an **English-language GPS** system (most cars come equipped, but ask just to be sure). If you'd rather use your phone for navigation, renting a **portable Wi-Fi device** is a good idea so you have a reliable internet connection throughout your trip, especially when heading to more rural areas.

Step 3: Rules, Road Conditions, and Parking

Driving in **Tokyo** can be a bit of a challenge due to traffic and limited parking, so it's generally best to avoid driving in the busiest parts of the city like **Shibuya** or **Shinjuku** unless necessary. In those areas, parking can cost **¥400 to ¥600 per 30 minutes**, and some hotels charge as much as **¥3,000 per night** for parking, so make sure to budget for that. There are apps like **Navitime** that can help you find parking spots in real-time, and when parking, always look for metered spots or designated lots. Never park on the side of the road unless it's clearly marked.

For longer trips outside the city, driving becomes much easier and more scenic. If you're heading out to **Hakone, Mount Fuji,** or even further to places like **Nikko,** you'll find parking much cheaper (around **¥500 to ¥800** for several hours) and roads much less crowded. Always check for toll roads—many highways, like the one to **Hakone,** have tolls that range from **¥2,000 to ¥3,000,** depending on your route. The easiest way to deal with these is to rent an **ETC (Electronic Toll Collection) card** when you get your car. This will allow you to pass through toll gates without stopping, and you'll pay for your tolls when you return the vehicle.

Step 4: Gas and Filling Up

Most rental will come with a full tank of gas, and you're expected to return the car with a full tank. Gas stations are easy to find across the city and in suburban areas, but many of them are full-service, meaning an attendant will fill your tank for you. A typical price for gas in Japan is around **¥150 per liter,** though it fluctuates slightly. Just ask for **"mantan"** (full tank) at the station, and the staff will know what to do. Credit cards are usually accepted, but it's always a good idea to keep some cash handy, especially in more rural areas.

Step 5: Rules of the Road

In Japan, cars drive on the left-hand side of the road. This might be different from what you're used to, so take extra care, especially when making turns at intersections. **Speed limits** in urban areas range from **40 km/h to 60 km/h,** while highways have limits between **80 km/h and 100 km/h.** Always follow the signs—they're clearly marked and consistent.

Be sure to yield to pedestrians—they have the right of way, especially at crosswalks, and Japanese drivers are generally very polite and respectful. Also, be aware that **driving under the influence** has a zero-tolerance policy in Japan, and penalties are very strict, including immediate suspension of your license. So if you're planning to drink, it's best to take public transport or use a taxi.

Step 6: Returning the Car

Head back to the same location where you picked it up unless you've arranged a different drop-off point in advance. Most rental offices, especially at **Haneda** and **Narita**, offer **shuttle buses** that will take you directly to the airport terminal after returning the vehicle. Make sure to allow a little extra time if you're catching a flight, just to be safe.

Step 7: Is Renting a Car Worth It?

While public transport in **Tokyo** is incredibly efficient, renting a car is ideal if you're planning a day trip or want to venture into the countryside. It's the perfect option for visiting **Mount Fuji**, **Hakone's hot springs**, or even taking a longer road trip to places like **Nikko** or the **Izu Peninsula**.

If you're thinking about food stops along the way, driving also gives you access to some amazing local eateries that are off the beaten path. In **Hakone**, for instance, you can stop at small roadside restaurants for **fresh soba noodles**, or if you're near **Fuji Five Lakes**, don't miss out on the local **Houtou noodles**. Just remember that parking near these attractions is easy and affordable, especially compared to central Tokyo.

CHAPTER 4
DISCOVER EACH DISTRICT

SHIBUYA

Shibuya is one of the liveliest areas. When you first get there, you'll likely be stepping out of **Shibuya Station**, which is right in the middle of the action. You'll want to take the **Hachiko Exit**. From here, you'll see the **Shibuya Crossing**—this is where you can experience one of the busiest pedestrian crossings in the world. It's really a sight to see, especially at night when the neon signs light up the whole area. If you want a good view, go to **Starbucks Tsutaya**, which is right there on the corner. Grab a drink, and you can watch the waves of people move across the intersection from a window seat.

Right by the crossing, you'll also find the **Hachiko Statue**. It's a famous meeting spot, and it's also a tribute to the loyal dog, Hachiko, who waited for his owner every day for years. It's easy to find—it's just a few steps from the station exit.

Once you've checked out the crossing and the statue, head to **Center Gai**, a street packed with stores, cafés, and fashion shops. You'll find it right off **Bunka-mura-dori**. This area is perfect for street shopping, and you'll see tons of trendy outfits and styles. If you're into fashion, make sure to stop by **Shibuya 109**, a super famous shopping mall that's all about youth fashion. It's right next to the station, so you can't miss it.

If you're looking for a break from all the shopping, you can walk to **Yoyogi Park**. It's only about a 15-minute walk from Shibuya Station. **Yoyogi Park** is one of the biggest parks in the city, and it's a great place to relax. On weekends, you'll often find performers and musicians hanging out there. During spring, the park is one of the best places for **cherry blossom viewing,** so if you're visiting then, grab some snacks from a convenience store nearby like **Lawson** or **7-Eleven** and have a picnic.

For food, you've got a ton of options. If you're craving sushi, check out **Uobei Shibuya Dogenzaka**, where you can get sushi from a conveyor belt. It's affordable too—about ¥100 to ¥300 per plate. It's just a 5-minute walk from **Shibuya Station**, on **Dogenzaka Street**. If you're in the mood for ramen, **Ichiran Shibuya** is a great place. You'll pay about ¥**1000 to ¥1200 for a bowl**, and it's perfect for a quick solo meal.

When it gets dark, Shibuya's nightlife kicks in. If you want to hit the clubs, **Dogenzaka** is where you'll find the best spots. Clubs like **Womb** and TK **Shibuya** are popular, and entry fees range from ¥3000 to ¥5000, depending on the night. But if you're looking for something more laid-back, head to **Nonbei Yokocho**, also known as **Drunkard's Alley**. It's a tiny alley filled with cozy, old-style bars, perfect for grabbing a drink in a more relaxed setting.

Getting around Shibuya is easy. The whole area is walkable, so once you're there, you don't need to worry about public transport. Just remember, if you're staying late, the last trains from **Shibuya Station** leave around midnight. If you miss the last train, taxis are available, but they can be expensive, starting at ¥730 for the first **1.2 km**. You'll find them lined up near the station.

SHINJUKU

Shinjuku is one of the busiest places you'll visit, and it's right in the heart of the city. It's easy to get to because **Shinjuku Station** is one of the main hubs, with lines like the **JR Yamanote Line** and the **Tokyo Metro** all stopping there. If you come out of the **west exit**, you'll be in the **Skyscraper District**. You'll see towering buildings, and a must-visit is the **Tokyo Metropolitan Government Building**, which is just **10 minutes on foot**. It has **free observation decks** where you can go up and see amazing views of the city, especially at sunset, and it's free to enter. It's open from **9:30 AM to 10 PM**.

If you head back toward **Shinjuku Station** and take the **east exit**, you'll walk straight into the busy area of **Kabukicho**, which is full of bright neon signs, restaurants, and entertainment spots. You can't miss the crazy **Robot Restaurant** here. It's a loud, flashy show with robots and performers, and it costs around ¥8,000. Kabukicho is also where you'll find bars, karaoke places, and all kinds of quirky things to do late at night. It's a good place to just wander around and take in the sights.

For something more old-school, check out **Golden Gai**, which is nearby. It's a bunch of tiny bars packed into small alleys, and each one has its own vibe. Some only fit about five people inside. Some bars may have a small cover charge of about **¥500-¥1,000**, but it's a unique experience, and the whole area feels very different from the big, busy streets around it. **Golden Gai** comes alive in the evening, so it's best to head there after **7 PM**.

When you need a break from all the action, walk over to **Shinjuku Gyoen National Garden**. It's about **15 minutes from Shinjuku Station** or a **5-minute walk from Shinjuku Gyoemmae Station** on the **Marunouchi Line**. This park is peaceful and beautiful, especially in spring or autumn, and it only costs ¥500 to enter. The park is open from **9 AM to 4:30 PM**.

For shopping, you've got to visit **Isetan**. It's a luxury department store, just a **5-minute walk from Shinjuku Sanchome Station**. They sell high-end fashion and have an amazing food section in the basement. You can grab lunch here for about **¥1,500-¥2,000**. If you're into ramen or street food, you can also head to **Omoide Yokocho**, just a **3-minute walk from Shinjuku Station**, where you can get **yakitori** (grilled chicken skewers) or ramen for **around ¥1,000-¥1,500**.

WHAT TO DO: SKYSCRAPER DISTRICT, NIGHTLIFE, ISETAN, ROBOT RESTAURANTS

In **Shinjuku**, you've got to dive into its **Skyscraper District**, where the famous **Tokyo Metropolitan Government Building** offers incredible panoramic views of the entire city. You'll find it at **2-8-1 Nishi-Shinjuku**, and it's open daily from **9:30 AM to 11:00 PM**. Best part? It's completely free. From the observation deck, you can gaze across **Tokyo's** sprawling skyline, and if you're lucky with the weather, you might even catch a glimpse of **Mount Fuji**. To get there, take the **JR Yamanote Line** to **Shinjuku Station**, exit from the **West Gate**, and it's just about a **10-minute walk**.

Once you've soaked in the cityscape, it's time to experience **Shinjuku's** bustling nightlife. Step into **Kabukicho**, located right near **Shinjuku Station's East Exit**, and this area is where **Tokyo's** neon lights are at their brightest. It's known as the city's most active entertainment district, packed with bars, quirky cafes, and countless izakayas. For something unforgettable, make a stop at the **Robot Restaurant** at **1-7-1 Kabukicho**. You'll find the entrance on **Godzilla Road**, famous for its massive **Godzilla head** perched above. The show is loud, flashy, and completely wild—it's not a traditional restaurant, but more of a futuristic spectacle with performers, robots, and lasers. Tickets cost about ¥8,000, and you can book them online or on-site. The showtimes vary, but you can usually catch it in the evening around **7:00 PM**.

Hungry or looking for a casual bite? A short walk from **Kabukicho** will take you to **Omoide Yokocho**, also known as "**Memory Lane**," located right off the **West Exit** of **Shinjuku Station**. This little alleyway is full of tiny eateries, mostly specializing in **yakitori** (grilled chicken skewers). You can grab a quick bite for around **¥150-¥200 per skewer**. It's a great spot if you're craving authentic, budget-friendly Japanese street food.

For drinks, **Golden Gai** is the place to be. This hidden network of narrow alleyways is packed with over **200 tiny bars**, each one seating just a handful of people. You'll find **Golden Gai** near **Kabukicho**, about a **5-minute walk** from **Shinjuku Station's East Exit**. The bars in **Golden Gai** are quirky and unique, with themes ranging from jazz music to movie posters. Drinks usually cost ¥700-¥1,000, but keep in mind many bars charge a **cover fee**, usually ¥500-¥800, especially for first-time visitors. **Golden Gai** starts buzzing after **8:00 PM**, making it an excellent spot for late-night.

And if shopping is on your list, make sure to visit **Isetan Shinjuku**, located at **3-14-1 Shinjuku**. It's a department store famous for its **depachika** (basement food hall) where you can find everything from sushi to fresh pastries and sweets.

The department store is high-end, but even if you're just browsing, the food hall is a must-see. You can easily spend ¥2,000-¥5,000 on gourmet food here, but it's well worth it. To get there, simply take the **Tokyo Metro Marunouchi Line** or **JR Yamanote Line** to **Shinjuku Station** and walk about **5 minutes** eastward.

AKIHABARA

Akihabara is the **epicenter of Japan's tech and anime culture**, with streets filled with electronics shops, video arcades, and anime stores that keep buzzing all day long. This district is located in **Sotokanda, Chiyoda City**, right by **Akihabara Station**. To get here, hop on the **JR Yamanote Line, Keihin-Tohoku Line**, or the **Tokyo Metro Hibiya Line**. The station is right at the heart of it all, making it super easy to jump straight into the action.

Akihabara Electric Town is where it all started. Originally famous for postwar electronics, it's now a haven for tech lovers. Start your journey at **Yodobashi Camera**, located just next to **Akihabara Station** at **1-1 Kanda Hanaokacho**, where you'll find **nine floors** packed with all the latest gadgets, from smartphones and cameras to PCs and home appliances. The prices here range widely based on what you're buying, so if you're looking to score deals, compare across floors or stores.

For **anime** and **manga** fans, **Mandarake** at **3-11-12 Sotokanda** is a **goldmine**. This eight-floor building is the **holy grail for collectors**, packed with vintage and rare anime items, manga, and action figures. You'll find limited edition collectibles, used manga, and cosplay outfits that are tough to get elsewhere. Prices range anywhere from ¥500 to ¥50,000 depending on rarity, so brace yourself. They also buy rare items, so if you've got collectibles you're ready to part with, Mandarake will take them off your hands.

Looking for **retro games**? **Super Potato**, located at **1-11-2 Sotokanda**, is a retro gamer's paradise. This quirky shop specializes in everything from **classic Famicom** consoles to **old-school cartridges** you might not have seen in decades. They even have a vintage **arcade** on the top floor where you can relive the glory days of gaming. Expect to pay around ¥2,000–¥10,000 depending on the rarity of the games you're looking for, and the nostalgia is free.

Club SEGA, at **1-11-11 Sotokanda**, is one of the most iconic. It's hard to miss with its giant neon sign, and once you step inside, it's all about flashing lights and buzzing machines. The place is packed with **rhythm games**, **fighting games**, and claw machines. Prices per game are usually around ¥100 to ¥500, and it's common to find people glued to the machines showing off their skills.

Now, **maid cafés** are something uniquely Akihabara. If you want a quirky, fun experience, **@Home Café** at **4-4-1 Sotokanda** is one of the most popular. Here, you'll be treated like royalty by waitresses dressed as maids, serving you food with elaborate presentations and cute gestures. Expect to spend around ¥1,500–¥3,000 for a meal and picture with a maid, and it's best to bring cash as some places might not accept cards.

For **anime-themed dining**, head to the **Gundam Café** right near **Akihabara Station**. Whether or not you're a fan of the iconic mecha series, the futuristic interior and themed menu are worth checking out. Dishes are around ¥1,200–¥2,500, and it's a perfect spot to refuel after exploring the area.

If you want a break from all the buzz, **Kanda Shrine**, also known as **Kanda Myojin**, is just a 15-minute walk away from **Akihabara Station**. This peaceful Shinto shrine has been around since the **Edo period**, and it's a surprising retreat from the tech chaos. You'll often find anime lovers visiting to buy charms, as the shrine has embraced the local culture, with special charms dedicated to electronic protection and anime-themed souvenirs.

Getting around is simple. The **JR Yamanote Line** or **Tokyo Metro Hibiya Line** can take you straight back to major spots in the city like **Shibuya** or **Ginza**. If you're planning on sticking around longer, Akihabara is also a short trip away from **Ueno** and its famous **park** and **museums**.

ASAKUSA

Asakusa is one of the most important spiritual spots in the city. You'll find **Senso-ji Temple** right at the heart of it, which is Tokyo's oldest temple. It's located at **2-3-1 Asakusa, Taito City** and is easy to reach by taking the **Tokyo Metro Ginza Line** or **Toei Asakusa Line** to **Asakusa Station**. It's a short walk from there, only about 5 minutes.

The temple is a huge attraction for both locals and tourists. You'll know you're in the right spot as soon as you see the massive **Kaminarimon Gate**. It's the entrance to the temple and is one of the most photographed places in the area. The giant red lantern in the middle of the gate is hard to miss. Once you walk through Kaminarimon, you'll be on **Nakamise Shopping Street**, a long path filled with shops selling traditional goods and snacks. This street is full of life, with small stalls offering local crafts like fans, dolls, and **kimonos**, and you can also try local sweets like **taiyaki** (fish-shaped cakes) or **melonpan** (sweet bread). Prices here vary depending on what you're buying, but you can expect to pay about **¥200-500** for street snacks.

At the end of Nakamise, you'll reach the **Hozomon Gate** which leads to **Senso-ji Temple** itself. The temple is free to enter, and it's open from **6:00 AM to 5:00 PM** daily, but the grounds are open 24/7, so you can walk around even after the temple's main hall closes. The temple was founded in **628 AD** and is dedicated to **Kannon**, the Goddess of Mercy. Inside, you'll see people performing the traditional offering ritual, where they toss coins, bow, clap, and then bow again. It's simple, but it's a special moment for many visitors.

While you're there, try drawing a fortune from the **omikuji** box near the temple. It's a fun and easy process: shake the container, get a numbered stick, and find the fortune that matches. If your fortune isn't great, just tie it to the metal racks nearby to leave the bad luck behind. This costs about **¥100** and is a cool way to participate in the local customs.

If you want to take a break after walking around the temple, **Asakusa Shrine** is just a short walk away. It's quieter and less crowded, making it a peaceful spot to relax. This shrine doesn't have an entry fee either, and you can visit it anytime during daylight hours.

For food, **Asakusa Imahan** is a great place to try traditional **sukiyaki**. It's located at **3-1-12 Nishi-Asakusa** and prices start around **¥2,500** for a meal. You can also snack on street food around the temple, like **menchi-katsu** (fried meat patties) or **dango** (sweet rice dumplings on skewers). These snacks usually cost between **¥200 and ¥400**.

GINZA

Ginza is **Tokyo's high-end shopping district**, and it's one of the most luxurious places you can visit in the city. If you're looking for luxury brands, **Chuo-dori Street** is the main hub, lined with flagship stores for names like **Chanel, Dior**, and **Gucci**. This is where you'll experience upscale shopping at its finest, with towering buildings filled with exclusive designer collections. You'll find **Mitsukoshi**, one of the most iconic department stores in Tokyo, right on **Chuo-dori**, at **4-6-16 Ginza, Chuo City**. The nearest station is **Ginza Station** on the **Tokyo Metro Ginza, Marunouchi, and Hibiya lines**, and you can get there by exiting at **Exit A11**.

Mitsukoshi is more than just a shopping experience; head down to the basement to the **depachika**, which is one of the best food halls in Tokyo. You'll find everything from gourmet sushi, delicate pastries, to intricately wrapped Japanese sweets. The **prices here can range from ¥1,000 for smaller snacks up to ¥10,000 for premium sushi**, but everything is a work of art. The building also has a **rooftop garden** where you can take a break and enjoy a peaceful moment away from the bustling streets below.

Ginza is also famous for its **Michelin-starred dining** options. One of the most renowned restaurants is **Sukiyabashi Jiro**, located at **Tsukamoto Sogyo Building, Basement Floor, 2-15 Ginza 4-Chome, Chuo-ku**. To dine here, expect to pay **around ¥40,000 per person**, and you'll need to **book months in advance**. Another standout is **Ginza Kojyu**, offering **kaiseki** (traditional Japanese multi-course meals) that cost **around ¥20,000 per person**. You can find Ginza Kojyu at **7-5-5 Ginza, Chuo City**, and the nearest station is **Ginza Station, Exit C2**.

Check out the **Pola Museum Annex** at **1-7-7 Ginza, Chuo-ku**, just a short walk from **Ginza-Itchome Station**. This **free museum** showcases rotating exhibits of contemporary art, making it a quiet and cultured escape from the shopping madness.

Ginza's history as a **luxury district dates back to the 1870s**, after it was rebuilt following a fire, which is when the area started to develop into a bustling commercial district. The famous **Wako Building**, with its distinctive **clock tower**, stands as a symbol of this blend of tradition and modernity. You'll find the Wako Building at **4-5-11 Ginza**, and it's one of the most photographed spots in the district.

The best time to explore is on **weekends**, when **Chuo-dori** becomes a **pedestrian paradise** from 12 PM to 5 PM, allowing you to stroll leisurely without the hustle of traffic. While walking, you'll notice a mix of **modern skyscrapers and old-school architecture**, giving Ginza a unique blend of the past and present. If you're hungry for a quick bite after all the luxury, there are numerous **French cafes** and **sushi bars** scattered around the area, offering everything from ¥1,000 **pastries to high-end meals costing ¥20,000 or more**.

The easiest way to reach Ginza is by taking the **Tokyo Metro Ginza Line** to **Ginza Station**. From there, **Chuo-dori** is just a short walk, and most major attractions in the area are accessible on foot within **5 to 10 minutes**. If you're arriving by train, you can also use the **JR Yamanote Line** and get off at **Shimbashi Station**, a 10-minute walk to **central Ginza**.

For parking, there are **paid parking lots** scattered throughout Ginza, but driving is not recommended due to the high traffic and expensive parking fees—about ¥400 **for every 30 minutes**.

WHAT TO DO

In Ginza is where you'll find some of the **world's top brands** and the kind of dining experiences that leave you amazed. Start with **Chuo-dori Street**, the main shopping strip where you'll see stores like **Louis Vuitton**, **Gucci**, and **Mitsukoshi**, one of Japan's oldest department stores. **Mitsukoshi** is located at **4-6-16 Ginza**, and it's not just for clothes shopping. The basement food hall, or **depachika**, is a must-see, offering gourmet treats, bento boxes, and even sushi. The prices range from ¥1,000 for snacks to much more for luxury food items. The store is open **10 AM to 8 PM** daily.

For art, stop by the **Pola Museum Annex** at **1-7-7 Ginza**, just a few minutes from **Ginza-Itchome Station**. This gallery is free and showcases modern Japanese art. You can spend around **30-40 minutes** here, soaking in a new exhibit each time you visit.

For lunch, treat yourself to a meal at **Sukiyabashi Jiro**, one of the most famous sushi restaurants in the world, located at **Tsukamoto Sogyo Building, Basement Floor, 2-15 Ginza 4-Chome**. It's pricey, about **¥40,000** for an omakase meal, but if you want to experience some of the best sushi, this is the place. If you can't get a reservation there, another option is **Ginza Kojyu**, a traditional **kaiseki** restaurant at **7-5-5 Ginza**, offering set meals that start at **¥20,000**.

After lunch, visit **Namiki-dori**, another major street filled with luxury boutiques. You'll pass by stores like **Hermès, Dior**, and **Chanel**. This street feels a bit more relaxed compared to the busier **Chuo-dori** and is perfect for a quiet luxury shopping experience.

In the afternoon, check out the **Shiseido Gallery** at **8-8-3 Ginza**. It's run by the famous cosmetics brand and has exhibits featuring experimental and contemporary art. The best part? It's free, so you can enjoy some culture without spending extra.

When it's time for dinner, you can't go wrong with **L'Osier**, a Michelin 3-star restaurant serving **French cuisine**. It's also located at **7-5-5 Ginza**, and meals here start around **¥12,000** for lunch. If you're more in the mood for a simple coffee break, try **Café de Ginza Miyuki-kan** for French desserts and coffee. Prices there are around **¥600 for a coffee** and **¥800 for their famous Mont Blanc cake**.

Ginza is equal to luxury, so take your time visiting the stores, art galleries, and restaurants. On weekends, the main street, **Chuo-dori**, is closed to cars from **12 PM to 5 PM**, so you can walk around freely. The nearest stations are **Ginza Station** on the **Ginza Line** or **Shimbashi Station** on the **JR Yamanote Line**, both within walking distance of all the action.

UENO: ART, MUSEUMS, AND TRADITIONAL MARKETS

You'll start in **Ueno Park**, one of the city's largest public spaces, surrounded by some of the most important **museums** in Japan. It's located in **Taito Ward** and can easily be accessed from **Ueno Station**, which is a major hub for both **JR lines** and the **Tokyo Metro**. Just exit via the **Park Exit**, and you'll be right there within a **5-minute walk** to the park itself.

Once inside **Ueno Park** (locally called **Ueno Onshi Koen**), which was originally the grounds of the **Kaneiji Temple** during the Edo period, you'll instantly feel the weight of history. This park was a key battleground during the **Boshin War** in 1868, and today, it's a green oasis filled with **cherry blossoms in the** spring, ponds, and, of course, the world-famous **Tokyo National Museum**. This museum, located on **13-9 Ueno Park, Taito City**, is a **treasure trove of Japanese art and history** and houses an incredible collection of over 100,000 objects. Expect to spend at least a couple of hours here if you're a history buff. The entry fee is **¥620** for adults, and the museum operates from **9:30 AM to 5:00 PM**, except Mondays when it's closed.

Art and Museums

After you've visited the **Tokyo National Museum**, you can head to the **National Museum of Western Art**, located just a **10-minute walk** across **Ueno Park**, famous for its works by **Monet, Rodin**, and other European masters. Admission is around **¥500**. Nearby, you've got the **Tokyo Metropolitan Art Museum**, known for contemporary exhibits, and the **National Museum of Nature and Science**, where you can immerse yourself in exhibits ranging from **dinosaurs** to **space exploration**. If you're interested in both art and science, this area is a goldmine.

Once you've had your fill of art and history, head down to **Ameya-Yokocho** (often called **Ameyoko**), a bustling street market just a **5-minute walk** from **Ueno Station**'s **Central Exit**. This market is a remnant of post-war Japan and offers everything from **cheap clothing, cosmetics**, and **fresh seafood** to **street food stalls**. For a quick bite, grab a **skewer of yakitori for about ¥150** or try some fresh **sashimi for ¥500**. The streets here are narrow and packed, so it's best to visit on weekdays in the late morning or early afternoon to avoid the heaviest crowds.

Eating Around Ueno

If you're still hungry after walking through **Ameya-Yokocho**, Ueno is filled with excellent eateries. **Izu-ei**, located at **2-12-22 Ueno, Taito**, is a famous **unagi (grilled eel)** restaurant where you can enjoy a traditional meal for around **¥3,000 to ¥5,000**. It's located just outside **Ueno Park**, making it a convenient stop. If you're in the mood for something sweet, check out **Kagetsudo** on the same street for its famous **melonpan**, a sweet bread that costs around **¥200**.

If you're looking to relax, consider visiting **Ueno Zoo**, Japan's oldest zoo located inside **Ueno Park**. The entrance fee is **¥600**, and you can see the **giant pandas**, which are a highlight, especially if you're traveling with kids. The zoo is open from **9:30 AM to 5:00 PM**, closed on Mondays. There's also **Shinobazu Pond**, where you can rent a paddle boat for a leisurely afternoon.

Getting to Ueno is straightforward from any part of Tokyo. The **JR Yamanote Line** will take you directly to **Ueno Station**, as will the **Tokyo Metro Ginza** and **Hibiya lines**. From **Tokyo Station**, the ride takes about **8 minutes**, and from **Shibuya**, it's around **24 minutes**. **Ueno** is also close to **Asakusa**, making it easy to combine both neighborhoods in one day if you have the energy.

HARAJUKU

Harajuku is located just outside **Harajuku Station** (which you can reach via the **JR Yamanote Line**) or the **Tokyo Metro** (on the **Chiyoda** or **Fukutoshin Lines** at **Meiji-Jingumae Station**), this narrow street is packed with trendy stores, vibrant street food, and a constantly moving crowd of young locals and curious tourists. It's best to visit on weekends when the street is at its liveliest, but be prepared for a packed experience, especially in the afternoons.

Walking down **Takeshita Dori**, the atmosphere is electric, and you'll immediately notice the mix of **Lolita fashion** and **vintage shops** lining the street. If you're into quirky or unique outfits, stop by **Bodyline** for some fun Lolita-style dresses or accessories. For vintage lovers, **Kinji Used Clothing** is a treasure trove of second-hand finds that can range from **¥2,000 to ¥10,000**, depending on what you're looking for. It's one of the best spots to pick up something one-of-a-kind without spending a fortune.

But **Harajuku** isn't just about fashion. **Cosplay** fans will be thrilled by the sight of groups dressing up in anime-inspired outfits, especially on Sundays when many gather to showcase their looks. Make sure to have your camera ready because this is one of the best people-watching experiences in Tokyo. If you want to immerse yourself deeper into **Harajuku's quirky culture**, pop into one of the **maid cafes** or **cosplay cafes** dotted around the area—one recommendation is **@home Cafe** located in the **Don Quijote building**, just a few minutes away.

Another must-try is **Harajuku's famous crepes**—a snack that's practically synonymous with this area. The most popular crepe stands are **Marion Crepes** and **Angels Heart**, both located on **Takeshita Street**. You can't miss their colorful storefronts and long lines of customers waiting to grab one of these sweet, rolled-up treats filled with ice cream, fruit, whipped cream, or even cheesecake. Prices are generally around **¥500 to ¥600**, depending on the toppings, and it's the perfect snack while you explore.

Now, if you're overwhelmed by the energy of **Takeshita Street**, just walk a little further to find peace at the **Meiji Shrine**, one of Tokyo's most famous Shinto shrines. The entrance is located just across from **Takeshita Dori** at **1-1 Yoyogikamizonocho, Shibuya**, and as soon as you pass under the massive **torii gates**, it feels like stepping into another world, far removed from the chaos of the city. The shrine was built in honor of **Emperor Meiji** and his wife **Empress**

Shoken and is surrounded by a serene forest that makes you forget you're in the middle of a metropolis. The shrine itself is free to enter, but you can also leave a wish or prayer on wooden **ema plaques** for ¥500, or buy a traditional charm for a similar price.

To complete your **Harajuku** visit, take a stroll down **Omotesando**, a broad tree-lined avenue just a short walk from **Takeshita Street**. This area is known for its more upscale vibe, offering luxury shopping, fancy cafes, and beautifully designed buildings. While the mood here is calmer, it's still quintessential **Harajuku**, blending the quirky with the sophisticated. You'll find **Omotesando Hills**, an elegant shopping complex filled with designer brands, as well as numerous **French-style cafes** perfect for people-watching or grabbing a coffee.

Harajuku can be reached quickly from **Shinjuku** or **Shibuya** by train, with **Harajuku Station** being the main stop. It's best to visit **between 11 AM and 4 PM** to catch all the action, but if you're looking to avoid the crowds, heading there early or later in the evening is a good idea.

To end the day with a bite to eat outside the crepe scene, just down the road on **Cat Street**, you'll find hidden gems like **Eddy's Ice Cream** or **Bills Omotesando** for a more relaxed atmosphere with great food, ranging from **¥1,000 to ¥3,000** for a meal. There's something for every kind of taste here in **Harajuku**,

HARAJUKU

Harajuku is located in the Shibuya area, and the main attraction here is **Takeshita Street**, the center of street fashion and pop culture in Tokyo. It's packed with colorful shops, small boutiques, and cafes, and you'll see a lot of unique outfits inspired by **Lolita fashion**—which is all about lace, ruffles, and Victorian-style dresses. The fashion on this street is wild and bold, and you'll spot some truly one-of-a-kind styles. Just hop off at **Harajuku Station** on the **JR Yamanote Line**, or take the **Tokyo Metro** and get off at **Meiji-Jingumae Station** to step right into the action.

Along Takeshita Street, you'll find everything from trendy accessories to full outfits in small shops like **Baby, The Stars Shine Bright**. If you want to dive deeper into the local pop culture, try a visit to one of the **cosplay cafes**, where the staff dress up as anime characters. **@Home Café** is a good one to check out. It costs about **¥500 to ¥1000** just to enter, and you can enjoy a fun, interactive experience with themed drinks and food.

There's also a huge focus on **vintage clothing** here. Stores like **Kinji Used Clothing** offer second-hand fashion at affordable prices—usually ranging from **¥1,500 to ¥5,000**—so if you're into thrifting, this is a great spot. After shopping, don't miss out on trying the famous **crepes** that are sold all along the street. Stands like **Marion Crepes** or **Angel's Heart** sell these tasty snacks filled with everything from strawberries to chocolate and whipped cream, for about ¥400 to ¥700.

When you've had enough of the hustle and bustle, walk over to the nearby **Meiji Shrine**, a peaceful spot hidden away in a lush forest just minutes from Takeshita Street. It's a **Shinto shrine** built in honor of Emperor Meiji and his wife, and it's completely free to visit.

SHIMOKITAZAWA

Shimokitazawa is located just a few minutes away from the hustle and bustle of Shibuya, and you can easily reach it by hopping on either the **Odakyu Line** or **Keio Inokashira Line** from Shibuya Station. It's just about a 5-minute ride on the Inokashira Line or around 7 minutes on the Odakyu Line. The popular stop for Shimokitazawa is **Shimokitazawa Station**, and the moment you step out of the station, you'll feel the laid-back, indie atmosphere that the area is famous for.

For vintage shopping, **Shimokitazawa** is a goldmine. Head straight to **New York Joe Exchange** on **Kitazawa Street**, about a 5-minute walk from Shimokitazawa Station. This unique store, once an old public bathhouse, offers a range of second-hand clothes, retro jackets, and accessories at prices from ¥1,000 to ¥8,000. If you love 70s or 80s fashion, another must-see shop is **Flamingo**—its racks are filled with funky dresses, patterned shirts, and statement pieces that reflect a bygone era. You can easily spend hours hopping from one vintage store to another, each with its unique charm.

Shimokitazawa's indie music scene is equally legendary. For a dose of live music, make your way to **SHELTER**, located on **Daiya Gai**—a 10-minute walk from the station. The shows here are intimate and give you a front-row experience with new bands. Expect ticket prices between **¥1,500 and ¥3,000**, depending on the event. For more underground vibes, head to **Basement Bar**, located near **Shimokitazawa Station**. It's one of the most well-known places in the indie scene, where you can catch live performances almost every night.

The cafes here are just as quirky and creative as the area itself. Stop by **Bear Pond Espresso**, which is located on **Kitazawa Street**. It's a small café known for its strong espresso that costs around ¥600, but trust me, it's well worth the price. For relaxed atmosphere, try **Café Stay Happy**, which offers a vegetarian-friendly menu with seating in hammocks, allowing you to kick back in true Shimokitazawa fashion. You can grab a meal for around ¥1,500.

Visiting Shimokitazawa doesn't stop with shopping or music; the small galleries and performance spaces add to its creative spirit. Check out **Suzunari Theater**, a cozy venue where you can catch everything from indie plays to live performances. It's located on **Suzunari Street** and ticket prices generally range from ¥1,000 to ¥3,000, depending on the performance. The area's love for arts and creativity is what makes every corner feel like a fresh discovery.

Food options are plentiful, with many local **izakayas** offering a casual dining experience. Try **Uoshin Izakaya** on **Suzunari Street** for fresh seafood; their sashimi and grilled fish dishes cost around ¥2,000 per person. If you're more in the mood for burgers, **Village Vanguard Diner** on **Daizawa Street** serves some of the best burgers in the area, with prices ranging from ¥1,200 to ¥1,800.

KOENJI

Koenji, located in the Suginami ward, west of central Tokyo, is a neighborhood famous for its **punk rock history**, retro charm, and alternative vibe. It's just **10 minutes away from Shinjuku** on the **JR Chuo Line**, with **Koenji Station** being the main hub for your visit. The atmosphere is relaxed but vibrant, attracting music lovers, vintage shoppers, and foodies looking for something more local than the bustling city center.

To get to Koenji, take the **JR Chuo Line** from **Shinjuku Station**—it's a quick ride, and you'll arrive in no time. If you're using the **Tokyo Metro**, **Shin-Koenji Station** on the **Tokyo Metro Marunouchi Line** is another option, which takes about **15 minutes** from **Shinjuku**. Either way, you'll find yourself in the heart of Koenji, ready to explore its **punk roots, retro shops, and indie music venues**.

PUNK ROCK AND INDIE MUSIC

Koenji's punk scene dates back to the **1970s**, when it became the epicenter of Tokyo's underground punk rock movement. Today, you can still feel that rebellious energy in its **live music venues** and dive bars. If you're a fan of punk and indie music, you won't want to miss **Koenji High** (located near the station at **2 Chome-1-9 Koenji Kita**). They host everything from punk and rock bands to indie gigs, with ticket prices generally ranging between ¥2,000 to ¥3,500.

Another venue worth checking out is **Club Mission's**, located a short walk away on **4 Chome-28-11 Koenji Minami**. This spot is famous for intimate performances, where you can get close to the stage and feel the raw energy of Tokyo's indie scene.

ALTERNATIVE SHOPPING AND VINTAGE STORES

Koenji is packed with **vintage stores**, making it a hotspot for thrift shopping. Start on **Pal Shopping Street**, just a few minutes from the station. Here, you'll find shops like **Spank!** and **Kiki2**, where quirky street fashion mixes with retro finds. Whether you're looking for a **1960s mod dress** or an **80s punk jacket**, there's always something to discover in these vintage havens. Prices range widely depending on the item, but you can score pieces for **¥1,000 to ¥5,000**. For lovers of rare finds, this is a dream.

FOOD

After some shopping, you'll want to grab a bite to eat. Koenji is known for its cozy, hidden eateries that serve up local flavors. Head to **Daikonman**, located on **Kita Koenji Street**, for **yakitori** (grilled chicken skewers). Prices are affordable, with skewers starting around ¥150, and the local atmosphere makes it a perfect spot to enjoy a casual meal. It's a great place to experience authentic Japanese food without the tourist traps.

For ramen, check out **MENYA Musashi**, located at **3 Chome-25-4 Koenji Kita**. Their **tsukemen** (dipping ramen) is highly recommended, with rich broth and thick noodles that cost around **¥900 to ¥1,200**. It's a hearty, satisfying meal that'll keep you going after a day of exploring.

NIGHTLIFE

Koenji's nightlife is all about **dive bars** and intimate, laid-back spots where you can enjoy a cheap drink. **Benny's Place**, located on **Koenji Street**, is one of those spots. With beers priced around ¥500, it's a no-frills place where locals and visitors mix, and the atmosphere is friendly and casual. If you're looking for something off the beaten path, this is the place to wind down your night.

Special Events: Koenji Awa Odori Festival

If you're visiting in late August, you're in for a treat. The **Koenji Awa Odori Festival** is one of Tokyo's most famous traditional dance festivals, drawing huge crowds to the streets of Koenji. The festival features **traditional Awa Odori dancers** parading through the streets, accompanied by live music and energetic performances. It's a vibrant mix of old and new, showing off both Koenji's **cultural heritage** and its modern-day **alternative edge**.

CHAPTER 5
HIDDEN GEMS

YANAKA: OLD TOWN

Yanaka is just a short walk from **Nippori Station** on the JR Yamanote Line, and it feels like stepping into Tokyo's past. The area is full of narrow streets, old wooden houses, and small, family-run shops that give it a charming, laid-back vibe far from the busy city center. Start your visit at **Yanaka Ginza**, the main shopping street filled with stores selling everything from handmade ceramics to traditional snacks. You'll love trying **taiyaki**—those fish-shaped cakes with red bean filling, usually around ¥150-¥200 each—and grabbing some **kibi dango**, little sweet rice dumplings for just about ¥100 each.

Walk a bit further, and you'll reach **Yanaka Cemetery**, which is especially stunning in spring when cherry blossoms cover the paths. It's a peaceful place, great for a quiet walk, and free to enter. The cemetery even has the grave of Tokugawa Yoshinobu, the last shogun of the Edo period, which adds a unique historical touch.

Close by is **Tenno-ji Temple** on Yanaka 7-chome, a lovely spot with a serene atmosphere and a big Buddha statue at the entrance. This temple has been here for centuries, and it's free to visit, making it an ideal place to take a break from walking and enjoy some quiet.

As you wander, take in the old Edo-style wooden houses and hidden temples around each corner. You'll find **Yuyake Dandan**, a set of steps near Yanaka

Ginza, is one of the best places to catch the sunset. At the end of the day, the light gives the street a golden glow, perfect for photos.

For a coffee break, try **Kayaba Coffee** nearby, which has been around since the 1930s and offers classic Japanese coffee shop items like toast for around ¥300 and coffee for about ¥500. If you're in the mood for a treat, **Himitsudo** is famous for its shaved ice (kakigori) in seasonal flavors, usually costing between ¥700 and ¥1200.

Getting here is easy. Take the **West Exit at Nippori Station**, follow signs toward Yanaka Ginza, and it's less than a five-minute walk. If you're already in Ueno, it's just a 10-minute bus ride or a 20-minute walk. Most shops close by 5 PM, so it's best to visit earlier in the day to explore at your own pace, try some snacks, and experience the peaceful, nostalgic atmosphere.

SHIMOKITAZAWA

Shimokitazawa, or "Shimokita" as locals call it, sits in Setagaya Ward, just west of the hustle in Shibuya and Shinjuku, but it has a totally different feel that makes it one of Tokyo's most beloved indie and artsy spots. Known for its free-spirited vibe, Shimokitazawa is packed with vintage clothing shops, music venues, and cafes that make you feel like you're in a hip, small town inside Tokyo.

To reach Shimokitazawa, take either the **Odakyu Line** or the **Keio Inokashira Line**, which is around a 5-10 minute train ride from Shibuya or Shinjuku stations. Get off at **Shimokitazawa Station**, which places you right in the middle of all the action.

Suzunari Street is one of the area's busiest spots and sets the tone with narrow lanes and boutiques lined side-by-side. Start by exploring vintage treasures at shops like **New York Joe Exchange** on **Kitazawa 3-chome**—it's a popular thrift store in an old bathhouse, and you'll find everything from trendy jackets to retro accessories here, with prices starting around ¥1000. For those after rare, curated finds, head to **Haight & Ashbury** on **Daizawa Street**; this store is known for its iconic vintage denim and unique pieces, with prices usually in the range of ¥3000-¥10000.

Shimokitazawa is also a massive hub for Tokyo's indie music scene, with venues that cater to rock, jazz, and experimental sounds. **Shelter**, located on **Kitazawa 2-chome**, hosts live shows almost nightly with tickets typically ranging from ¥2000-¥3500. Shows usually start around 7 p.m., but the vibe here is best when the place fills up with a crowd that's all about the music. For a more intimate setting, check out **Club Que** on **Shimokitazawa Station Street**, which has been around for decades and has seen some of Japan's best underground acts.

When you're ready to recharge, Shimokitazawa doesn't disappoint with its lineup of cafes and eateries. For an authentic espresso experience, visit **Bear Pond Espresso** on **Kitazawa Street**, where you can get one of Tokyo's best espressos for about ¥500. Or, for a unique vibe, swing by **Shimokitazawa Cage**— an open-air space with food stalls, pop-up shops, and events on **Daizawa Street**. It's perfect for a laid-back afternoon hangout.

If you're in the mood for a wander, let yourself get lost in Shimokitazawa's maze of streets. You'll stumble across countless second-hand bookshops, record stores, and cozy, tucked-away eateries. For lunch or dinner, try **Oishi Komachi Shokudo** on **Suzunari Street**, a beloved spot for Japanese home-style meals, where you can get a satisfying dish for around ¥1000.

Plan to spend at least half a day here, especially if you're visiting on the weekend, as Shimokitazawa hosts various pop-up markets that bring local vendors out onto the streets. Most shops open around **11 a.m.**, and if you're into live music, plan to stay into the evening.

KOENJI

Located just west of **Shinjuku** on the **JR Chuo Line**, you'll find this neighborhood only about a 10-minute train ride from **Shinjuku Station**. Step out at **Koenji Station**, and you're instantly in a world where Tokyo's past meets its edgy, rebellious side. The best time to start exploring is around late afternoon; Koenji transforms as the sun sets, with its music scene and nightlife gradually coming alive.

First, walk along **Pal Shopping Street**, a vibrant stretch filled with vintage clothing stores, record shops, and bars tucked into narrow, gritty alleyways that are teeming with character. The area is famous for its **indie boutiques** and vinyl stores—don't miss **Disk Union Koenji** (just off **Koenji Street**), where rare punk and rock albums line the shelves. Another treasure, **Spank!**, on **Look Street**, offers quirky, colorful vintage finds straight from the '80s and '90s, with prices ranging around ¥3000-¥8000, making it ideal if you're on the hunt for truly unique fashion statements.

Koenji's music scene is intense and authentic, still pulsing with the punk energy it's known for. Check out **ShowBoat** on **Koenji Kitaguchi Street** for live shows nearly every night, where entry fees run from ¥2000-¥3500. Expect anything from gritty rock bands to experimental indie artists, creating an underground vibe that captures Koenji's soul. And if you're ready to dive into the bar scene, **Dachibin**, a cozy spot on **Koenji Station Street**, is a local favorite, known for its laid-back, welcoming atmosphere, and cheap drinks around ¥500. Not far from there is **Bar Garaku** on **Koenji South Street**—small, lined with vinyl records, and filled with locals who know their music.

For food, Koenji excels in **street food and izakayas** that keep things affordable. Along **Daruma Street**, you'll find stalls offering classic Japanese eats like skewers, takoyaki, and small grilled dishes. For a sit-down meal, head to **Manmaru** on **Koenji South Street**, where you can enjoy Osaka-style okonomiyaki for about **¥800-¥1500** per dish. The vibe is casual, loud, and always filled with regulars.

A hidden gem within Koenji is **Za Koenji Public Theatre** on **Koenji North Street**. While it may not immediately scream punk rock, this theater is known for avant-garde and experimental performances, and if you're around during a festival, you might catch something truly unique. Tickets typically cost **¥2000-¥5000** depending on the show, and it's a local recommendation for anyone interested in Tokyo's alternative arts scene.

NEZU SHRINE

Is located specifically along **Nezu Street**, this ancient shrine has been here since the **Edo period**, when it was rebuilt by the Tokugawa Shogunate. Steeped in over **1,900 years of history**, the shrine draws visitors not just for its architecture but also for its peaceful gardens and iconic **vermilion torii gates** that create a serene, otherworldly atmosphere as they wind through the lush grounds.

The best way to reach Nezu Shrine is by hopping onto the **Tokyo Metro**

Chiyoda Line and getting off at **Nezu Station** (Exit 1), which places you just a 5-minute walk away along **Shinobazu Street**. If you're coming from Ueno, it's just two stops away, making it easily accessible within Tokyo's central neighborhoods. If you're using the **Namboku Line**, you can get off at **Todaimae Station** and enjoy a pleasant 10-minute stroll to the shrine. Be sure to check transport timings if you're visiting early to avoid any rush-hour crowding; the **Tokyo Metro** typically runs every few minutes throughout the day.

Once inside, start your visit by exploring the **tunnel of red torii gates**, a unique feature of the shrine where each gate stands vibrant against the surrounding greenery. The best time for photographs is around late morning or early afternoon when the light plays beautifully with the shadows along the torii path. Continue on to the **main hall** for a glimpse of traditional Japanese shrine architecture, and don't forget to visit the **Azalea Garden** during its bloom season from late April to early May. Entry to the garden during the Azalea Festival costs about ¥200, and the vivid pinks and purples of the flowers make the shrine look like a scene straight out of a painting.

Around the shrine, you'll find plenty of spots to stop for traditional snacks. Look out for vendors selling **mitarashi dango**—small, skewered rice dumplings grilled and coated in a sweet soy glaze. You can grab a stick for around ¥150, making it an affordable and authentic taste of Japan. If you have a little more time, you might want to stop by **Kayaba Coffee** on Yanaka Street for a relaxed tea or coffee break in a cozy setting that has retained its old Tokyo charm.

If you are interested in local crafts, the **Yanaka Ginza** shopping street is just a short walk away. Here, you'll discover artisan shops, handmade goods, and small family-run businesses that sell everything from pottery to sweets, all capturing the quaint and nostalgic spirit of Tokyo's old neighborhoods. This

TODOROKI VALLEY

Todoroki Valley, known as Tokyo's only gorge within the city, is a lush, serene escape located in **Setagaya Ward**, just a short distance from Todoroki Station on the **Tokyu Oimachi Line**. This hidden gem is perfectly reachable within a **5-minute walk from Todoroki Station**—just head down **Todoroki 1-chome** street toward the valley entrance, where a small path starts your journey into greenery.

Once inside, you're greeted by the **Yazawa River**, a gentle stream that meanders through the valley, guiding you along winding, stone pathways under a canopy of trees. One of the first highlights you'll reach is the **Todoroki Fudoson Shrine**, a shrine dating back to the **Edo period**. This shrine is easy to spot with its traditional red bridge and serene surroundings that invite quiet reflection. It's home to a series of intricately carved statues and features like the **Fudo-no-Taki Waterfall**, a small but serene waterfall believed to purify visitors and add to the calming atmosphere of the place.

For walkers, plan on a **20- to 30-minute leisurely stroll** through the valley, but keep in mind that there's no rush—this spot is ideal for simply unwinding. Best times to visit are early mornings or weekdays when you can enjoy the quiet without the crowds, and the seasonal changes add to the beauty: **cherry blossoms** paint the valley in spring, while **autumn leaves** bring vivid colors in the fall.

As for places to rest or eat nearby, look for **Setagaya Park Café** on **Setagaya-Dori Street**, offering a casual ambiance with light meals, ideal for a quick coffee or a bite after your walk. Alternatively, head to **Bistro La Cave**, located just minutes from the valley's exit, for a heartier meal in a cozy setting—meals here range around **1,500 to 2,500 JPY**. For a taste of Tokyo's local flavors, **Todoroki Monja**, located near Todoroki Station, is perfect for sampling monjayaki, a savory pancake famous in Tokyo, with prices around **1,000 JPY per person**.

Getting there is straightforward: take the **Tokyu Oimachi Line from Shibuya Station** directly to Todoroki Station in about 15 minutes. Trains run frequently, with one every 5-10 minutes, making it easy to plan your visit. The valley itself is open to the public without entry fees and closes at dusk, so make the most of the daylight and enjoy the refreshing escape right in the heart of the city.

HOW TO FIND THESE HIDDEN GEMS

Yanaka: Tokyo's Old Town Serenity Take the **JR Yamanote Line** to **Nippori Station**—it's just a 20-minute trip from Tokyo Station, costing around ¥160. **Yanaka** is where you step back in time, with narrow lanes filled with old wooden shops, cozy cafes, and street vendors selling traditional snacks. Head straight for **Yanaka Ginza**, a lively shopping street where you'll find taiyaki and handmade ceramics. Walk along **Yomise-dori Street**, where you can get a feel for how Tokyo looked before the skyscrapers took over. Stop by the **Yanaka Cemetery**—especially beautiful in cherry blossom season.

Shimokitazawa: The Indie Scene Hop on the **Keio Inokashira Line** from Shibuya or the **Odakyu Line** from Shinjuku (each ride costs around ¥160), and within 10 minutes, you're in **Shimokitazawa**, a mecca for indie culture and alternative vibes. It's packed with retro clothing shops, music venues, and cafes. Try **Flamingo** or **Haight & Ashbury** for standout vintage finds, and check out live music at **Shelter** or **Basement Bar** if you're craving that underground Tokyo sound. For a chill coffee break, **Bear Pond Espresso** has a laid-back vibe.

Todoroki Valley: Tokyo's Green Sanctuary Catch the **Tokyu Oimachi Line** from Shibuya, get off at **Todoroki Station** (25 minutes, around ¥180). This green escape runs along Todoroki Gorge, where the river flows quietly beside tree-shaded paths. Walk straight into the valley and follow the nature path along the river—pure relaxation. You'll find a small tea house along the way, where you can stop for a refreshing cup of matcha before climbing up to **Todoroki Fudo Temple** for great views and a peaceful moment. Nearby cafes have light snacks and coffee, perfect to wrap up your stroll.

Nezu Shrine: Spiritual Tokyo Take the **Chiyoda Line** to **Nezu Station** (10 minutes from Tokyo, ¥170). **Nezu Shrine** is known for its beautiful red torii gates and azalea garden, which comes alive in spring. Walk through the torii gate tunnel to the main shrine, where you can visit the traditional architecture and the beautiful garden. It's free to enter, and you'll get an amazing photo-op, especially in the early morning when it's quiet. Follow shrine etiquette—bow before entering the main hall, wash hands at the purification fountain—and enjoy the calm. Afterward, local wagashi shops nearby have perfect sweet treats to enjoy with matcha.

CHAPTER 6
FOOD

FOOD CULTURE

Japanese dining is about respect for the food and the chefs. **When you step into a restaurant in Tokyo, give a small bow to show respect, and if you're in a traditional spot, you'll probably need to remove your shoes right at the door**—you'll see a shelf or lockers by the entrance for this, and some places provide slippers, so slip those on before walking in.

When ordering, some ramen shops have **ticket machines at the entrance— just pick your meal on the screen, pay, and hand over the ticket to staff**. In other places, call out "Sumimasen" (excuse me) to get the server's attention. **The right phrases matter here—saying "Gochisousama deshita" as you leave shows you appreciated the meal**, and it's something restaurant staff truly value.

Japanese dishes come with a little etiquette of their own. **For sushi, take the piece in one bite, with minimal soy sauce to respect the chef's seasoning**; with ramen, feel free to slurp—it's totally fine and shows you're enjoying it! **Tempura is served hot and crispy**, and the quicker you eat it, the better it is.

Tokyo's street food keeps things easy and tasty. **Try takoyaki, which are round octopus balls with a crispy outside and a hot, gooey center topped with bonito flakes**. Taiyaki, a fish-shaped pastry, is usually filled with sweet red bean paste, custard, or chocolate. And yakitori—grilled chicken skewers—are a perfect street bite and often paired with a cold beer in an izakaya, or Japanese pub.

In upscale restaurants, stay quiet, avoid adding extra soy sauce unless it's

served, and savor each bite in a calm setting. In ramen shops, izakayas, or casual sushi spots, you can chat and enjoy, but avoid crossing chopsticks or passing food between them—little details like this matter here.

Paying is easy—just head to the register on the way out, as tips aren't expected, so thank you is enough.

BUDGET EATS

Ameya-Yokocho Market in Ueno is your go-to for cheap, tasty street food. Just hop off at **Ueno Station** on the JR Yamanote Line and walk to **Ameyoko Street**, which is close to Ueno Park. Open from around 10 a.m. till evening, you'll find snacks like **takoyaki (octopus balls)** for about ¥300 and **taiyaki** (fish-shaped pastries with sweet red bean) for around ¥200. For the best experience, head there in the early afternoon when it's lively, and you'll get fresh bites without too many people.

Isetan in Shinjuku and Mitsukoshi in Ginza have great food basements (depachika) where you can pick up affordable, fresh Japanese food. These spots are easy to reach—**Isetan's near Shinjuku Station and Mitsukoshi's near Ginza Station**. Inside, find bento boxes with sushi, tempura, and sides starting at **¥500-¥1,200**. Sushi stalls, grilled skewers, and desserts are everywhere. Most depachika open at 10 a.m. and close by 8 p.m. If you're in Shinjuku, bring your food over to Shinjuku Gyoen National Garden, and in Ginza, try Hibiya Park, both just short walks away.

For fresh seafood that's affordable, **Tsukiji Outer Market** is a must. It's close to **Tsukijishijo Station** on the Toei Oedo Line. You'll find **kaisendon (seafood bowls)** for around ¥1,000-¥1,500, along with tamagoyaki (sweet omelet) for about ¥100-¥200 each. Go early, like 7-8 a.m., to catch the freshest seafood before it gets crowded. After eating, explore the market streets to see the seafood culture up close.

In **Shinjuku**, Memory Lane (also called Omoide Yokocho) right by **Shinjuku Station's West Exit** has small yakitori and ramen places that fill the alley with smoky smells of grilled meat. Yakitori skewers are about **¥150 each**, and a bowl of ramen costs around **¥800-¥1,000**. It's best to go from 5 p.m. until midnight when the lights are on and everything's lively. Once you're done, Kabukicho and Golden Gai are nearby, perfect if you want to explore the nightlife.

Tokyo's convenience stores (konbini) like **7-Eleven, Lawson, and FamilyMart** have surprisingly great food. You'll find them everywhere, and they're open 24/7, so they're perfect for snacks anytime. Onigiri (rice balls) are around ¥100-¥150, sandwiches are ¥200-¥300, and bento boxes are as low as ¥300. You can find them in places like Akihabara and Ginza, perfect for quick snacks while you're visiting.

DEPACHIKA RECOMMENDATIONS: ISETAN SHINJUKU, MITSUKOSHI GINZA

In Tokyo's food halls, or *depachika*, like **Isetan Shinjuku** and **Mitsukoshi Ginza**, you'll find a ton of amazing Japanese food, all set up in a way that makes it easy to explore and try new things. To reach *Isetan Shinjuku*'s depachika, just head to **Shinjuku Station's East Exit** and then walk five minutes to **Shinjuku-dori Avenue**. This place is open from *10:00 AM to 8:00 PM*, so you've got plenty of time to look around and sample different foods. Inside, you'll find a huge variety, from **fresh sushi and bento boxes** to **tempura** and **Japanese sweets**. Typical sushi trays start around ¥1,000, with some fancier options up to ¥2,500. If you're just grabbing a snack, **rice balls** (onigiri) are around ¥200 to ¥500 each and come filled with classics like **tuna, seaweed, or salmon**. Definitely try the **tempura**— crispy shrimp or veggies that they fry fresh for you.

At *Mitsukoshi Ginza* on **Chuo-dori Avenue**, you get a similar vibe with a more high-end touch, especially since it's in **Ginza**. Take the **A11 exit at Ginza Station**, and you're there. They open at **10:30 AM and close at 8:00 PM**. Here, you'll find **fancier sushi and sashimi bowls, French-Japanese pastries**, and **wagashi sweets**. Sushi sets range from about ¥1,500 to ¥3,000, while **traditional sweets** go for around ¥500 to ¥700 each, especially the **matcha-flavored treats** that are unique to Japan and worth a try. The **pastries** are a must too, mixing

Japanese and French styles, making for a perfect snack if you're spending the day in Ginza.

If you go early, like in the morning or right after lunch, it's less crowded, and you'll have a full selection of everything. *Cash is good to have* since some stalls take cards, but paying with cash is often quicker. Start with small things like **onigiri** or **sweets** so you can taste a bit of everything without filling up too fast. And, if you want to sit somewhere to enjoy your finds, you've got great options nearby. After you visit **Isetan**, *Shinjuku Gyoen National Garden* is about a fifteen-minute walk away, perfect for a quiet picnic with your food hall goodies. In **Ginza**, *Hibiya Park* is a seven-minute walk from Mitsukoshi and is also a great spot to sit and enjoy your treats in a relaxed setting right in the middle of the city's busy vibe.

DINING MID-RANGE

Ippudo Ramen in Shibuya is the perfect place if you're craving ramen that's both rich and filling. Just a short walk from **Shibuya Station's Hachiko Exit** on **Dogenzaka Street**, it's open **from 11 AM to midnight**, so you can head there any time for lunch, dinner, or a late-night bite. Expect to spend around ¥800 to ¥1,200 for a bowl of ramen with a creamy broth, chewy noodles, and delicious pork chashu. The vibe is casual, perfect for relaxing.

For a fun and affordable sushi spot, check out **Genki Sushi** on **Udagawacho Street** in Shibuya. This place is minutes from **Shibuya Station** and has a fun conveyor-belt setup where you order on a touch screen and get your food delivered on a little "train." Plates go for around ¥100 to ¥200, so you can try different kinds without worrying about cost. They're open from **11 AM to 11 PM**, but go during the early afternoon if you want to avoid crowds. Try the salmon nigiri, tuna, or the fusion rolls for something different.

In Shinjuku, **Torikizoku** on **Yasukuni Dori Street** is a top choice if you want a cozy izakaya experience without spending too much. Located close to **Shinjuku Station's East Exit**, it's open **from 5 PM to midnight**, and almost everything on the menu, from grilled chicken skewers to drinks, is **around ¥300**. For a real Shinjuku vibe, check out **Omoide Yokocho** nearby, also known as "Memory Lane." It's a little alley packed with izakayas and yakitori spots, and you'll get that retro, authentic feel of old-school Tokyo.

Another ramen spot worth trying is **Ichiran Ramen** in Shinjuku, right on **Kabukicho Street**. It's open **24/7**, so it's great for late-night or early-morning ramen cravings. You get to customize your ramen flavors here, and it's usually

¥1,000 to ¥1,200 per bowl. Plus, they have individual booths, which makes for a cool, focused experience on your ramen.

To get to any of these spots, take the **Tokyo Metro or JR Yamanote Line** to either Shibuya or Shinjuku stations. It's easy to find them they usually have English menus or picture guides, so ordering is simple.

EXAMPLE RESTAURANTS: IPPUDO RAMEN, GENKI SUSHI

Ippudo Ramen in Shibuya is all about ramen. Is located on **Dogenzaka Street**, this spot is easy to reach—just a short five-minute walk from **Shibuya Station's Hachiko Exit**. The ramen here has a creamy pork broth that's been simmered for hours, giving it a deep, savory flavor. The classic bowl, which usually costs between **¥900 and ¥1,200**, comes with tender chashu pork, a soft-boiled egg, and perfectly cooked noodles. Add a side of gyoza (pan-fried dumplings) for **¥300-¥500** if you're hungry; they're crispy on the outside and juicy inside. This area around Dogenzaka has lots to explore, with cool shops and the famous Shibuya Crossing just steps away, so you can really make a whole afternoon or evening of it. Take the **Tokyo Metro or JR Yamanote Line** to Shibuya Station; trains come frequently, and it's super easy to find.

If you're in the mood for sushi, head to **Genki Sushi on Udagawacho Street**, also just minutes from Shibuya Station. Here, you'll get a fun and modern sushi experience with their unique conveyor belt setup that brings each dish straight to your table. You use a tablet to order, so it's easy even if you don't know much Japanese. Prices are really affordable, with plates usually between **¥100 and ¥300**, so you can try different types without spending too much. The seared salmon, with just a touch of soy sauce, is a favorite for many, so don't miss it. Genki Sushi is open from **11 AM to 11 PM**, and getting there early in the evening helps you avoid the crowds. It's a short walk from Shibuya's Hachiko Exit, making it easy to visit more of the area right after you eat, like checking out the famous shops and entertainment nearby.

To get to both spots, use the **Tokyo Metro or JR Yamanote Line to Shibuya Station**. The trains are frequent and convenient, and the walk to each restaurant is short and straightforward.

FINE DINING

Sukiyabashi Jiro is legendary and sits right in Ginza, on **Ginza Street**, a luxury area known for high-end shopping and sophistication. To get here, take the **Tokyo Metro Ginza Line to Ginza Station** and use exit C6, which will bring you just a short walk away. This sushi experience, led by Chef Jiro Ono, known worldwide and featured in documentaries, offers you sushi pieces served one by one, each crafted with over 50 years of expertise. Meals start around ¥30,000 per person and reservations are essential—book months ahead if possible. When you finish, you're steps away from iconic stores like **Mitsukoshi** and **Wako Department Store** for a luxurious stroll afterward, adding even more to this exclusive Ginza experience.

Then there's **Narisawa**, located in the **Minami-Aoyama** district at **2 Chome-6-15**, known for its cutting-edge blend of Japanese ingredients and French culinary techniques. Narisawa is closest to **Omotesando Station** (accessible via the Ginza, Chiyoda, and Hanzomon lines), and from here, it's a comfortable 10-minute walk along charming, tree-lined streets. Chef Yoshihiro Narisawa's dishes mirror the seasons, and the menu changes frequently to match the landscapes of Japan. Expect to pay between **¥25,000 to ¥40,000**. For a relaxing end to your meal, head to nearby **Omotesando Hills** for coffee, or stroll along **Cat Street** to explore boutique shops and art galleries.

For traditional kaiseki dining that feels deeply rooted in Japanese culture, **Kikunoi Akasaka** offers an exquisite experience located at **6-13-8 Akasaka**. Just a 5-minute walk from **Akasaka-Mitsuke Station** on the Ginza and Marunouchi Lines, this serene, beautifully designed restaurant feels like a peaceful retreat amid Tokyo's bustle. Chef Yoshihiro Murata presents a seasonal menu, with each course telling a story tied to Japan's culinary history. Meals here range between **¥20,000 to ¥35,000**. Afterward, walk over to **Hie Shrine** for a quiet exploration of one of Tokyo's famous Shinto shrines or visit the **Tokyo Midtown** complex nearby for a blend of shopping and art.

For a modern and playful twist, try **Den** in **Jingumae**, a short walk from **Gaienmae Station** on the Ginza Line, nestled in the lively **Shibuya-Ku** area. Located at **2-3-18 Jingumae**, Chef Zaiyu Hasegawa's creations bring a fresh, surprising take on Japanese cuisine that is both high-end and fun, with touches that make each dish unique and memorable. Expect to spend around **¥23,000 to ¥28,000** per person. Once you finish, you're right by **Aoyama Cemetery** for a peaceful walk or the bustling **Omotesando** area for more trendy cafes and shops.

VEGETARIAN, VEGAN, AND HALAL FOOD

In **Shinjuku**, start with **Ain Soph Journey** on Shinjuku 3-Chome. Located a few steps from **Shinjuku Sanchome Station**, this spot is ideal if you're near Shinjuku's bustling shopping areas or visiting places like Shinjuku Gyoen National Garden. You'll find all-vegan meals, from creamy curries to well-loved vegan pancakes. Expect to pay around **¥1,500 to ¥2,500 per person**, with lunchtime being particularly popular, so try to go early in the day. The cozy interior makes it a great spot to recharge before heading out to explore Shinjuku's highlights.

For vegan ramen in central Tokyo, head to **T's TanTan** inside **Tokyo Station** on Keiyo Street. Tokyo Station is a prime hub for travelers, so if you're stopping by the station for the Shinkansen or exploring Marunouchi, make sure to stop here. Their signature ramen options, like spicy sesame or soy-based broth, are all vegan, and meals here usually cost **¥900 to ¥1,100**. With quick service and a relaxed atmosphere, it's a perfect meal stop while navigating Tokyo Station's massive layout.

If you're looking for halal yakiniku, try **Gyumon** in Shibuya on Shibuya 3-Chome. Just a short walk from **Shibuya Station** and close to the famous Shibuya Crossing, it's an ideal spot to unwind after sightseeing in Shibuya. Here, you'll enjoy a halal-certified yakiniku experience with beef and chicken options grilled right at your table. Prices generally range from **¥2,500 to ¥4,000 per person** depending on your choice of cuts, and you'll find the ambiance both traditional and friendly.

Sekai Cafe in Asakusa is a fantastic option if you're exploring Asakusa's rich cultural sites, like Senso-ji Temple or the Nakamise Shopping Street. It's located on Asakusa 1-Chome and offers a mix of halal and vegetarian-friendly dishes, from veggie burgers to light Japanese dishes, and meals are usually around **¥1,000 to ¥2,000**. The café has a relaxed, inviting vibe, making it perfect for unwinding after visiting the temples and markets of Asakusa.

If you're near Ueno, look for **Nataraj** on Ueno 2-Chome, which serves vegetarian and vegan Indian food, offering an entirely plant-based experience with flavorful curries and naan. Located close to **Ueno Station** and near Ueno Park, it's a convenient stop if you're spending the day around Ueno Zoo, Tokyo National Museum, or Ameya-Yokocho Market. Expect a meal to cost around **¥1,200 to ¥2,000 per person**. This spot is popular among locals and visitors alike, so consider arriving early or during off-peak hours to get a table without a wait.

VEGAN-FRIENDLY CAFES: AIN SOPH, T'S TANTAN

Ain Soph Journey is one of Tokyo's standout vegan spots, located in **Shinjuku 3-Chome**, just a short walk from **Shinjuku-Sanchome Station**, which is accessible via the **Tokyo Metro Marunouchi Line** or **Fukutoshin Line**. If you're heading here, take Exit C3 from the station, and you'll find yourself a five-minute stroll from this cozy oasis tucked into the bustling Shinjuku district. Ain Soph Journey opened in 2009 with a mission to create hearty, flavorful meals that go beyond typical vegan fare, giving plant-based diners a fulfilling, memorable meal with a touch of elegance.

Their opening hours are **11:30 a.m. to 9:00 p.m.** on weekdays and weekends, but try to get there early during lunch to avoid the crowds, as it's a favorite spot among locals and travelers. Expect to pay around **¥1,500 to ¥2,500** for mains like their signature veggie burger, which comes with a side of crispy fries and fresh salad, or their creamy mushroom pasta topped with fragrant herbs. If you're in the mood for something sweet, the fluffy pancakes are a must-try, generously topped with seasonal fruit and maple syrup.

The atmosphere is laid-back, with warm lighting and earthy decor that makes you feel like you're in a little retreat away from the busy streets outside. Beyond just food, Ain Soph is also known for its warm and welcoming staff, who are always happy to help you navigate the menu if you're new to vegan cuisine in Japan.

T's TanTan, on the other hand, is located inside the **Tokyo Station** building, on Keiyo Street, making it incredibly convenient if you're commuting or sightseeing in the area. To reach it, just head toward the **Yaesu South Exit** inside Tokyo Station and follow the signs for Keiyo Street. Since it's right in the heart of the station, it's hard to miss, and it's open daily from **7:30 a.m. to 11:00 p.m.**, which makes it a perfect spot to grab breakfast, lunch, or dinner. This restaurant is known for pioneering vegan ramen in Japan, bringing rich flavors and hearty broths to a plant-based audience, and the focus here is on recreating traditional Japanese ramen but in a totally vegan-friendly way.

Prices here are around **¥900 to ¥1,100** per bowl, with options ranging from their classic sesame-based ramen to more adventurous flavors like spicy tantan-men. Be sure to try the vegan gyoza on the side for an extra bite of flavor. The atmosphere is vibrant and casual, with a steady stream of locals and tourists, and it's a great spot if you're craving something quick, hearty, and authentically Japanese without worrying about animal ingredients.

For those exploring Tokyo's broader vegan scene, consider visiting areas like **Shibuya** or **Harajuku**. These neighborhoods have a variety of plant-based cafes, from pop-up spots to more established eateries. Harajuku, with its trendy Takeshita Street, is particularly known for quirky vegan ice cream spots and smoothie stands, while Shibuya offers more cafes with wholesome, vegan-friendly menus.

To make finding vegan-friendly places easier, you can download apps like **HappyCow**, which list vegan and vegetarian spots with reviews, or ask for "ビーガン" (biigan) for vegan options and "菜食" (saishoku) for vegetarian options to help navigate menus.

UNIQUE DINING

Mameshiba Cafe is located on **Takeshita Street** in **Harajuku**, known for its quirky youth culture. It's a short walk from **Harajuku Station** on the **JR Yamanote Line**. Open daily from **11 AM to 7 PM**, you can step inside for about **¥880** per person for a 30-minute session. The atmosphere here is relaxed as Shiba Inu dogs roam freely among guests, making it ideal for a break from the busy shopping streets nearby. The cafe's popularity skyrocketed due to Japan's love for pets and the laid-back ambiance unique to Tokyo. You can grab a coffee, and if you're lucky, the dogs might come for a pet or sit near you, making for a calming, joyful experience.

Calico Cat Cafe in **Shinjuku** offers a similar escape, with hours running from **10 AM to 10 PM** daily. Located near **Shinjuku Station's East Exit**, it's just a five-minute walk away. This cat cafe charges about **¥1,000** for the first hour, with prices adjusted for longer visits. The cafe has a large variety of cats lounging around, often peeking out from high shelves or cozy corners. A visit here gives you the chance to enjoy Tokyo's famous cat cafe culture, which emerged from the country's apartment lifestyle and limited space for pets at home. The calming environment makes it perfect for unwinding after a long day visiting Shinjuku.

For a pop-culture twist, **Kawaii Monster Cafe** in **Harajuku** delivers a full neon-fantasy experience. Located close to **Meiji-jingumae Station** on the **Tokyo Metro** (Chiyoda Line), the cafe is open daily from **11:30 AM to 4 PM** for lunch and **6 PM to 10:30 PM** for dinner. The decor is eccentric, with neon lights, oversized sculptures, and rainbow-colored walls, matched by colorful food like rainbow pasta and flashy drinks. A meal here typically costs **¥2,000 to ¥3,000**, making it a perfect spot to experience Japan's colorful, whimsical culture without stepping into a themed show. The Kawaii Monster Cafe reflects Tokyo's "kawaii" or cute culture, which has deep roots in the Japanese love for playful and exaggerated aesthetics.

Robot Restaurant in **Kabukicho**, Shinjuku's entertainment hub, offers a visually striking and high-energy experience. Just a five-minute walk from **Shinjuku Station**, it's open from **3 PM to 10 PM** with performances throughout the day. Tickets cost about **¥8,000**, though discounts are often available online. Meals here are light, as the main attraction is the futuristic robot show—giant robots, lasers, and dancers fill the stage with an overload of sensory experiences. This spot captures Tokyo's tech-savvy and playful side, a reminder of Japan's innovation streak and love for vibrant, immersive entertainment.

For a retro experience, **Maidreamin Cafe** in **Akihabara** offers another layer of Tokyo's unique pop culture. Located a short walk from **Akihabara Station** on the

JR Yamanote Line, it's open from **11 AM to 10 PM**. Expect to spend around ¥1,500 to ¥2,500 depending on the meal and any add-ons, like a Polaroid photo with a maid. Here, waitresses dressed in maid costumes serve dishes with playful decorations, drawing hearts on your omelet with ketchup. This trend emerged in the early 2000s as a subculture for fans of anime and gaming, and Maidreamin has since become one of the most popular in Akihabara's thriving pop culture district.

The **Golden Gai** area in **Shinjuku** is perfect if you're in the mood for an authentic Tokyo night. Located near **Shinjuku Sanchome Station** on the **Tokyo Metro** (Marunouchi Line), this network of narrow alleyways is filled with tiny bars and izakayas, many no bigger than a single room. Open from **8 PM to late** into the night, you'll find small plates of yakitori, sashimi, and local drinks, often for around **¥2,000 to ¥3,000**. Each bar has its own distinct personality, some with vintage records, movie posters, or quirky decor reflecting the owner's personality. The area's charm lies in its intimacy, which developed post-WWII and has since preserved Tokyo's retro nightlife scene.

For something different, head to **Kurand Sake Market** in Ikebukuro. Near **Ikebukuro Station's East Exit**, it's open daily from **5 PM to 11 PM** and offers an all-you-can-drink sake tasting experience for about **¥3,000**. This spot lets you sample various sake from across Japan, all self-served, so you're free to try as many as you like at your own pace. You can also bring your own food to pair with the drinks or try their small snack options. This market highlights Japan's deep-rooted sake culture and provides a fun, social way to discover different varieties of the traditional Japanese drink.

CHAPTER 7
DAY TRIPS FROM TOKYO

HAKONE

For a good day trip to **Hakone**, you have to start by getting the **Hakone Freepass**, which provides access to almost all local transport options, including the **Tozan Railway**, cable cars, and even a scenic cruise on **Lake Ashi**. You can buy this pass at Odakyu stations like **Shinjuku Station**—from Shinjuku, it's 5,700 yen, and if purchased in Hakone, it's around 4,600 yen. The **Odakyu Romancecar** express train from Shinjuku to **Hakone-Yumoto Station** is highly recommended for comfort, costing an additional 1,110 yen each way and taking about 85 minutes.

Once in Hakone, you have to start by visiting **Lake Ashi** for beautiful views of **Mount Fuji** and the iconic red torii gate of **Hakone Shrine** along the lake's shore. The **Hakone Sightseeing Cruise** on the lake is covered by your Freepass and takes around 30 minutes. For a traditional lunch, try **Oshino Soba** along the lakefront, where a bowl of soba noodles will set you back around 1,200 yen.

Next, you have to go to the **Hakone Open-Air Museum**, located along the **Tozan Railway**. Open daily from 9 a.m. to 5 p.m., the museum charges an entry fee of 1,600 yen, but it's absolutely worth it for the mix of nature and art, especially in the **Picasso Pavilion**.

After soaking in some art, it's time to relax at **Hakone Yuryo Onsen**, conveniently located near **Hakone-Yumoto Station**. Here, a traditional Japanese hot spring experience is set in serene wooded surroundings. Entry is approximately 1,500 yen, and you can book a private bath if you prefer. Just remember, it's Japanese custom to rinse off thoroughly before entering the hot spring to show respect and maintain cleanliness.

For one last stop, take the **Hakone Ropeway** to the **Owakudani Valley**. The ropeway, also included in the Freepass, provides a panoramic view of the valley's volcanic activity, with steam vents and sulfurous clouds making it a unique experience. The ride takes around 30 minutes and, on clear days, offers more views of **Mount Fuji** from above. Try the local specialty, **kuro-tamago** (black eggs), cooked in the hot sulfur springs; these eggs are said to add seven years to your life, and you can find them in small stalls near the ropeway station for about 500 yen per pack.

To make the most of your day in Hakone, aim to arrive by 9 a.m. and avoid weekends to miss the crowds.

GETTING THERE

To get from Tokyo to Hakone easily, **start at Shinjuku Station** on the Odakyu line. Look for the **Odakyu Romancecar**, a direct, comfortable train that takes you straight to **Hakone-Yumoto Station** in about **85 minutes**. This train is great if you want a scenic view, as the big windows give you a great look at the mountains and sometimes even Mount Fuji. Tickets are around **2,300 yen one-way**, and that includes a reserved seat, so no stress about crowded cars. Buy tickets at the **Odakyu Sightseeing Service Center in Shinjuku** or online to make sure you get a spot, especially if you're going on a weekend.

For traveling around Hakone itself, get the **Hakone Freepass**. This pass covers all your local travel in Hakone and includes the **Hakone Tozan Railway, cable cars, ropeway, buses**, and even the **pirate ship cruise on Lake Ashi**. If you're starting in Shinjuku, the Freepass is about **5,700 yen**, which covers your round trip and all the transport inside Hakone. If you're already in Hakone, you can get a local version for **around 4,600 yen**. You can pick it up at Odakyu stations, like Shinjuku, and it makes getting around super simple.

Once you reach **Hakone-Yumoto Station**, you're at the main gateway to Hakone. From here, take the **Hakone Tozan Railway** up to **Gora Station**. The train twists up a steep hillside, passing through thick trees and mountain views. At **Gora**, switch to the **Hakone Cable Car** going up to **Sounzan Station**, and then hop on the **Hakone Ropeway**. This ride gives you a bird's-eye view over Owakudani, a volcanic valley known for its sulfur hot springs. There, try the famous black eggs, boiled in the hot springs and said to add years to your life if you eat one. You can find these eggs for around **500 yen**.

The Ropeway will also take you to **Lake Ashi**, where the **Hakone Pirate Ship** cruise awaits. This ship, included with your Freepass, is fun and has the best views of Mount Fuji and the mountains, especially during autumn. Close by, **Hakone Shrine** with its red torii gate in the lake is a must-see. To reach the shrine, head to **Moto-Hakone Port** after your lake cruise; it's just a short walk from there.

If you're feeling hungry, try the eel restaurant on **Yumoto Chaya Street** for fresh, local flavors, or **Tamura Ginkatsutei** near Gora for their famous tofu cutlets, which cost about **1,200 yen**. At the **Hakone Open-Air Museum**, which has amazing outdoor sculptures and even a hot spring foot bath, you can grab snacks or coffee at nearby cafes. Entry to the museum is about **1,600 yen**.

The **Odakyu Romancecar departs every 30 minutes from Shinjuku**, so it's easy to time your return to Tokyo as late as you like, letting you fully enjoy Hakone's hot springs, lakes, and amazing views.

NIKKO

Start to Nikko at Asakusa Station in Tokyo, where you'll find **Tobu Limited Express SPACIA trains,** the quickest and most direct route to **Tobu-Nikko Station.** Departures are frequent, and you can expect to arrive in Nikko in about **two hours. Tickets cost around 2,800 yen each way,** or grab the **Tobu Nikko Pass for approximately 4,500 yen,** which covers your round-trip journey and includes unlimited bus rides around Nikko's main attractions. You can buy this pass right at Tobu counters in **Asakusa or Ikebukuro stations**.

Once at **Tobu-Nikko Station** on **Higashiyama Street,** head straight to **Toshogu Shrine,** a **UNESCO World Heritage site** about **15 minutes away by bus** or taxi. Buses leave from the station regularly, and you can use your Nikko Pass to cover the fare. The **shrine entry fee is around 1,300 yen,** and it's worth every bit for the opportunity to see this sacred site, which houses the remains of **Tokugawa Ieyasu, founder of the Tokugawa shogunate. Look for the Yomeimon Gate,** intricately adorned with carvings of flowers, birds, and mythical creatures, and don't miss the Three Wise Monkeys carving that has come to symbolize "see no evil, hear no evil, speak no evil." If you're hungry after exploring, grab a quick bite of **yuba (tofu skin),** Nikko's specialty, at one of the local stalls nearby, where it's served in soups, rice bowls, and more.

From Toshogu, hop back on a local bus to **Kegon Falls,** one of Japan's highest waterfalls at 97 meters, located near **Lake Chuzenji.** You can take an elevator down to the base for **570 yen,** and if you're visiting in autumn, you'll get to see stunning fall colors surrounding the falls. While here, explore **Lake Chuzenji,** a calm, clear lake formed from volcanic activity, and enjoy the lakeside walk or rent a boat for a different perspective. If you want to grab lunch nearby, try some **grilled trout** or **sweetfish,** common local dishes often served at small eateries around the lake.

For hikers, Nikko offers trails for all levels in **Nikko National Park.** A beginner-friendly hike near **Mount Nantai** offers scenic forest paths, while more advanced hikers can explore **Odashirogahara Marshland** with its open fields, wildflowers, and distant mountain views. Most trails are well-marked, and you'll find maps available at major starting points like **Senjogahara Plateau** near Lake Chuzenji.

At the end of your day, **head back to Tobu-Nikko Station** to catch the **Limited Express SPACIA** back to Asakusa. The last trains usually leave around **5:30 p.m.,** so plan accordingly to ensure a smooth journey back.

KAMAKURA

To visit Kamakura fully, you have to start by taking the **JR Yokosuka Line from Tokyo Station** to **Kamakura Station**. The ride is about **an hour** and costs **940 yen one way**, with frequent trains running every **15-20 minutes**. Once you arrive, begin with **Kotoku-in Temple** on **Hase Street**, home to the iconic **Great Buddha** statue, or **Daibutsu**, crafted in the **13th century**. From Kamakura Station, hop on the **Enoden Line to Hase Station** (a five-minute ride), followed by a **10-minute walk** along Hase Street, where you'll pass traditional shops and eateries along the way. Entry to the temple is **300 yen**, with a small **20 yen fee** if you want to step inside the Buddha statue. This monumental bronze statue is surrounded by peaceful gardens and scenic temple grounds that make for a serene start to the day.

Continue to **Hasedera Temple**, a **five-minute walk from Kotoku-in**. The temple is known for its **eleven-headed Kannon statue**, nearly **10 meters tall**, and its beautiful **hydrangea path** that blooms with color in early summer. The views of Kamakura's coastline from here are breathtaking, especially if you head to the upper garden terraces. The **entry fee is 400 yen**, with gates open from **8:00 am to 5:00 pm** in most seasons. This temple has both historical significance and scenic beauty, giving you a perfect mix of Kamakura's nature and spiritual heritage.

Next, go to the **Kamakura Beach** near **Yuigahama Station** on the **Enoden Line** (one stop from Hase). This beach, stretching along the coastline, is a local favorite for sunbathing, surfing, and taking leisurely walks. You'll find small food stands where you can grab local snacks like **kakiage (vegetable tempura)** on rice or **shirasu-don**, a bowl of rice topped with fresh whitebait, costing **800-1,200 yen**. The beach offers a laid-back vibe, and it's ideal for people-watching or a picnic, with locals relaxing by the shore and surfers catching waves.

End the day with a visit to **Tsurugaoka Hachimangu Shrine**, Kamakura's main Shinto shrine, located at **2 Chome-1-31 Yukinoshita**, about a **10-minute walk from Kamakura Station**. Founded in the **12th century**, this shrine is Kamakura's spiritual center, surrounded by ancient trees and lined with traditional lanterns. It's free to enter, and the main hall offers scenic views over Kamakura. Walking through the shrine's long path lined with trees and seasonal flowers adds a serene finale to your day. The best time to visit is early evening when the shrine is lit up, casting a beautiful glow over the area.

When you're ready to head back to Tokyo, take the **JR Yokosuka Line from Kamakura Station** to Tokyo Station. The last train runs late, giving you flexibility to enjoy Kamakura's charm.

MOUNT TAKAO

To reach **Mount Takao**, head to **Shinjuku Station** and look for the **Keio Line** bound for **Takaosanguchi Station**; a one-way ticket costs **around 390 yen** and takes **about 50 minutes** to reach the base of the mountain. If you're starting earlier in the day, trains run frequently, so catching one between **8 and 9 a.m.** gives you plenty of time to enjoy a full day on the trails. Takaosanguchi Station, located on **Uratakao-machi, Hachioji**, is the ideal stop since it drops you right at the base of the mountain trails.

Once there, you'll find signage guiding you to **Trail 1**, the most popular and accessible route, offering paved paths leading up to the summit. Trail 1 has stops like **Yakuoin Temple**, where centuries-old statues and temple structures allow for quiet reflection or photos along the way. The trail is lined with viewing points that are especially popular in **autumn**, usually **late November**, when the trees burst into vibrant reds and yellows. Expect this path to take around **90 minutes to 2 hours** at a leisurely pace.

For who is looking for a quicker ascent or an alternative way to experience the climb, head to the **cable car station**, located just a **5-minute walk from Takaosanguchi Station**. The cable car, which costs around **490 yen one way** or **950 yen round trip**, climbs halfway up, letting you bypass the steeper sections and giving you more time to explore the upper trails. This is also a great option if you're traveling with younger children or prefer a more relaxed way up.

At the summit, which is roughly **599 meters high**, you'll find an observation deck with sweeping views over Tokyo, and on clear days, **Mount Fuji** can often be seen rising majestically in the distance. The summit area has several small eateries where you can grab a bowl of **soba noodles for about 600 yen** or try **yakitori skewers**. **Recommended** for an authentic snack is **Mount Takao's famous dango** (rice dumplings) with sweet soy glaze, available from food stalls right at the summit for around **300 yen**.

If you're up for a scenic yet peaceful route, **Trail 6** is another option, winding through denser forest alongside a small stream and taking you up over several shaded paths—perfect if you're seeking tranquility or a more secluded experience. This trail leads up to **Inariyama Ridge**, where the elevation offers more dramatic views and fewer crowds compared to Trail 1.

YOKOHAMA

Take the the **JR Tokaido Line** or **JR Yokosuka Line** from **Tokyo Station**, with trains departing every few minutes and taking around **30 minutes** to reach **Yokohama Station**. A one-way fare is about **470 yen**. Once you arrive, Yokohama opens up with an impressive mix of modern attractions.

Begin at **Minato Mirai 21**, a waterfront district where Yokohama's skyline meets the ocean. From Yokohama Station, you can hop on the **Minatomirai Line** to **Minato Mirai Station**, a 3-minute ride that brings you close to some of the city's top attractions. Minato Mirai 21 is known for **Landmark Tower**, Japan's second-tallest building, located on **Minatomirai Boulevard**. For a beautiful experience, go up to the **Sky Garden Observation Deck** on the 69th floor for a fee of around **1,000 yen**. Here, you'll enjoy 360-degree views that extend to Mount Fuji on clear days. This modern district is also lined with shopping centers like **Queen's Square** and **MARK IS**, where you can take a break at trendy cafes or take a look at Japanese fashion boutiques.

Nearby is the **Cup Noodles Museum**, a quirky and interactive stop on **Shinko 2-chome** where you can learn about the history of instant noodles, a Japanese innovation. Open daily from **10 a.m. to 6 p.m.** (closed Tuesdays), it offers exhibits on the life of Cup Noodles' creator, Momofuku Ando, as well as a chance to design your own cup noodles for **400 yen**. It's a hands-on, creative experience that makes for great memories and a fun food souvenir.

Just a short walk away, you'll find the **Yokohama Red Brick Warehouse** on **1 Chome-1 Shinko**. Originally used for customs in the early 20th century, this historical building now serves as a shopping and cultural complex where you can find seasonal goods, locally made items, and artisanal food stalls. It's also a great place to sample some of Yokohama's unique culinary offerings, like **Yokohama-style shumai (dumplings)**. The warehouse is open from **10 a.m. to 8 p.m.**, and it's especially atmospheric in the evening when the historic brick walls light up.

A visit to **Yokohama Chinatown** is a must, located a few minutes away from **Motomachi-Chukagai Station** on the Minatomirai Line. Known as one of the largest Chinatowns globally, it offers a vibrant array of food stalls, bakeries, and traditional Chinese shops along **Yamashita-cho**. You can try popular snacks like **nikuman (steamed buns)** or stop by one of the many Chinese-Japanese fusion restaurants. Many food items here range from **300 to 600 yen**, making it an affordable and flavorful stop. Chinatown is especially lively during the Lunar New Year or other Chinese festivals, when the streets come alive with parades and decorations.

For a peaceful escape, head to **Sankeien Garden** at **58-1 Honmoku Sanno-tani**, an expansive Japanese garden that's a perfect contrast to the busy harbor. To get here, take a local bus from Yokohama Station to Sankeien in about **35 minutes** for **220 yen**. Entry to the garden costs **700 yen**, and it opens from **9 a.m. to 5 p.m.** The garden features winding paths, traditional teahouses, and scenic ponds, along with seasonal flowers that make it beautiful year-round—cherry blossoms in spring and vivid maple leaves in autumn.

End the day with a peaceful walk along **Yokohama Bay**. Near **Cosmo World**, a small amusement park with the **Cosmo Clock 21 Ferris wheel**, you can take in the bay views, especially beautiful at sunset. A ride on the Ferris wheel costs **800 yen**, providing a great perspective of the entire Minato Mirai district lit up in the evening.

PLANNING A DAY TRIP

To make the most of your day trip planning, **start at Tokyo Station** or **Shinjuku Station** early in the morning, ideally around 7 or 8 a.m., so you can enjoy a full day without feeling rushed. If you're going to **Hakone**, head to Shinjuku Station and pick up the **Hakone Freepass** at the Odakyu Sightseeing Service Center, located right in the station. This pass costs about ¥5,700 if you're traveling round-trip from Tokyo, and it covers your transportation within Hakone on buses, trains, and even boats on **Lake Ashi**. It also lets you access stops like the Hakone Open-Air Museum and Owakudani, the volcanic valley known for its sulfur springs and scenic views. Plan to visit the Hakone Open-Air Museum, an outdoor art space filled with sculptures, at ¥1,600 per adult and located near **Chokokuno Mori Station** on the Hakone Tozan Line.

For a day in **Nikko**, the **Nikko Pass** will cover your round-trip train from Tokyo plus access to main attractions like the **Toshogu Shrine**, famous for its intricate carvings and historical significance as the resting place of Tokugawa Ieyasu, and **Kegon Falls**, one of Japan's most famous waterfalls. You can buy the Nikko Pass at Tokyo Station for around ¥4,600 and it includes entry discounts. The train ride takes roughly two hours, so plan to leave early if you want to explore the surrounding nature or the temples. In the town center, you'll find cozy spots for local soba noodles and yuba (tofu skin) dishes, which make for a traditional and affordable lunch option, usually costing between ¥800 and ¥1,200.

For a coastal escape, **Kamakura** is a fantastic choice, accessible in under an hour by train from Tokyo. At Kamakura Station, start by visiting the **Great Buddha at Kotoku-in Temple**, which costs around ¥200 and is an iconic symbol of Kamakura's historical charm. Next, head to **Hasedera Temple** for beautiful garden views and, if you're there in summer, the blooming hydrangeas. A stroll along **Kamakura Beach** for a sunset view completes the experience. Trains back to Tokyo run frequently, but you might want to reserve a seat during peak hours to avoid crowds.

If you're heading to **Yokohama**, take the **JR Tokaido Line** from Tokyo Station; it's around 30 minutes to **Yokohama Station**. Here, you can explore the **Minato Mirai** district, with its futuristic architecture and waterfront views, or visit **Sankeien Garden**, a traditional Japanese garden about a 20-minute bus ride from Yokohama Station (entrance is about ¥700). Yokohama's **Chinatown** is a top spot for a variety of street food, from steamed buns to bubble tea, with prices usually under ¥1,000. The **Cup Noodles Museum** nearby provides an interactive experience, where for ¥500 you can even design your own noodle cup to take home.

For **Mount Takao**, leave from **Shinjuku Station** via the **Keio Line** directly to

Takaosanguchi Station in under an hour, with tickets priced around ¥390 one-way. This mountain is known for its accessible hiking trails and seasonal beauty, especially during autumn when the leaves are at their peak. If you prefer not to hike the entire way, take the cable car, which costs about ¥480 each way and brings you halfway up, from where you can enjoy panoramic views and, on a clear day, even catch a glimpse of Mount Fuji. At the summit, try some tenguyaki, a popular snack shaped like the mountain's folklore tengu spirit, priced around ¥150.

Bring a portable Wi-Fi device or download offline maps; as you may know already, apps like **Navitime Japan** and **Hyperdia** are great for checking train times, routes, and costs. For lunch, you can grab a bento box from station depachikas or try local specialties depending on your destination.

CHAPTER 8
THROUGH THE SEASONS: FESTIVALS, FOLIAGE, AND FIREWORKS

SPRING

C herry blossom season is one of the most magical times, and knowing exactly where to go makes all the difference if you want that perfect hanami experience. To start, head to **Ueno Park**, one of the city's most popular cherry blossom spots, located close to **Ueno Station** on the JR Yamanote Line, so it's super easy to reach by train. Once you're there, you'll be surrounded by over 1,000 cherry trees along the main paths and lakes. This spot gets really lively, so if you want a quieter experience, try to visit in the early morning. There are also tons of food stalls lining the pathways with tasty options like yakitori, takoyaki, and sweet taiyaki, each costing around **200 to 500 yen**, giving you an easy way to snack and enjoy a bit of Japanese street food under the blossoms.

Another incredible cherry blossom viewing location is **Shinjuku Gyoen**, right in the heart of **Shinjuku**, which you can reach by getting off at **Shinjuku-sanchome Station** on the Marunouchi Line. Shinjuku Gyoen opens at **9 a.m.** with an entry fee of about **500 yen**, and once you step inside, you'll find over 1,500 cherry trees spread across different garden styles, including Japanese, English, and French landscapes, each offering beautiful spaces for hanami. This is one of the best places for a relaxing and scenic walk with far fewer crowds, and it's also great if you're looking for those picturesque scenes with sakura trees around spacious, green lawns. Since the weather can be cool in spring, especially in the morning and evening, be sure to bring some layers and a blanket if you plan to sit on the grass for a while.

For another spot head to **Chidorigafuchi**, which is the area around the **Imperial Palace moat**, easily accessible from **Hanzomon Station** on the Hanzomon Line. Here, you can rent a rowboat for around **800 yen** for **30 minutes**, allowing you to float beneath the cherry blossoms hanging over the water, which creates a really dreamy and magical scene that's perfect for photos. If you prefer to stay on land, you can walk along the paths beside the moat, where the cherry trees form beautiful archways overhead, and there are also food stalls nearby with snacks and drinks to keep you refreshed as you stroll.

Since cherry blossoms are only in full bloom for about a week, you'll want to check Tokyo's cherry blossom forecast, which usually shows peak bloom between late March and early April, and checking it right before you go can help you plan for the best timing. Spring weather can vary, so make sure to have a light jacket, especially for cooler mornings and evenings.

SUMMER: FESTIVALS, FIREWORKS, AND BEATING THE HEAT

Summer festivals bring out a lively side of the city that's impossible to miss, with colorful celebrations, fireworks, and dances that fill the streets. These festivals have been celebrated for many decades, and each one has its own history and cultural significance.

The **Sumida River Fireworks Festival**, one of Tokyo's most anticipated events, takes place every year on the last Saturday of July along the **Sumida River**, close to **Asakusa**. This massive display of fireworks goes back to the Edo period (18th century) and was initially held as a way to lift spirits during times of hardship. Now, it's a celebration of summer and a beloved annual tradition. To get there, take the **Ginza Line to Asakusa Station** or the **Hanzomon Line to Oshiage Station**; both stations are just a 10-minute walk from the river. The fireworks start around **7 p.m.** and last until **8:30 p.m.**, but arriving as early as **3 p.m.** is wise to get a spot along the riverbank. You'll find endless food stalls offering classic festival snacks like **yakitori** (around **300 yen**), **takoyaki** (**400 yen**), and **chilled beer** (**500 yen**), perfect for an evening of fireworks. People from all over Japan come to see this show, so expect crowds and bring a **mat or blanket**, **fan**, and **portable charger** for your phone or camera.

Another summer highlight is the **Bon Odori Festival**, where people gather in parks and plazas throughout Tokyo to perform traditional dances honoring the spirits of ancestors. The **Hibiya Park Bon Odori** near **Hibiya Station** on the Hibiya Line is popular, bringing hundreds of people every August for dances that go back centuries. You'll find food stalls and small shops selling **traditional fans and yukata** (summer kimonos) if you'd like to dress up. The Shinjuku Eisa Festival, held in **Shinjuku's main shopping area near Shinjuku Station**, also honors Okinawan culture with energetic drum dances that fill the streets with rhythm. Most of these festivals are free to attend, and stalls around the park sell **yakisoba** (fried noodles, around **500 yen**) and **kakigori** (shaved ice, around **300 yen**), ideal for cooling off.

One of the most unique summer celebrations is the **Asakusa Samba Carnival**, an event that turns Asakusa into a lively, Brazilian-inspired street party every late August. This festival began in the 1980s and has since become a huge attraction, drawing thousands of visitors to **Asakusa-dori Street**, right by **Asakusa Station** on the Ginza Line. Dancers dressed in vibrant costumes parade through the streets, creating a fun mix of Japanese and Brazilian cultures. It's best to arrive by **12 p.m.** to get a good viewing spot. You'll find plenty of snacks nearby, like **grilled squid** or **fruit skewers** (300–400 yen each), so you can easily grab something on the go.

Festivals are incredibly popular and deeply rooted in Japanese tradition. Most of them run annually and bring people together from all over Japan, making summer one of the best times.

AUTUMN

You have to visit the **Rikugien Garden** in Bunkyo City is one of top spots for autumn foliage, offering a beautiful look at Japanese garden landscaping combined with fiery autumn colors that really peak around **mid-November**. You'll find this garden near **Komagome Station** on the JR Yamanote Line or the Tokyo Metro Namboku Line, just a short walk down **Honkomagome Street**. Entry costs **300 yen**, and the garden is open from **9 a.m. to 5 p.m.** daily, though in peak season, they extend hours for a special evening illumination that lights up the trees until closing. Arriving in the **late afternoon** is perfect, so you can capture the trees both in daylight and under the evening lights. The garden also offers tea houses where you can enjoy traditional matcha and sweets while taking in the view, a relaxing spot for a break as you stroll. **Packing a light jacket** is smart for evening visits since temperatures dip quickly as the sun sets.

Meiji Jingu Gaien, famous for its **Icho Namiki Avenue** (Ginkgo Avenue), sits near Harajuku and Omotesando and creates a golden pathway lined with vivid yellow ginkgo trees in the heart of **Minato Ward**. You can get here by taking the Tokyo Metro Ginza Line to **Gaienmae Station**; it's just a short walk along **Aoyama Street**. The best time to visit is typically **late November** for peak colors, and it's free to walk along the avenue, though for a more scenic view, visiting mid-morning gives you the best lighting without too many crowds. You'll find small cafes and food stands along the route selling seasonal treats like **yakiimo** (roasted sweet potatoes) and chestnuts, perfect for snacking as you wander beneath the golden leaves. If you're craving a sit-down spot, there are cozy cafes nearby on **Aoyama Street** where you can enjoy a coffee with the autumn scenery.

For something with a cultural twist, **Hibiya Park** near **Hibiya Station** on the Tokyo Metro Hibiya Line hosts the **Tokyo Chrysanthemum Exhibition** each November, celebrating the Japanese art of **kiku** (chrysanthemum) shaping. The park, located on **Hibiya Koen Street** in **Chiyoda Ward**, transforms into a floral paradise with chrysanthemums displayed in various traditional arrangements. Admission is generally free, and the park is open **24 hours**, though the exhibition is best enjoyed during daylight for its vibrant colors. Nearby, you can grab a bite at one of the small restaurants along **Sotokanda Street** offering seasonal dishes that reflect autumn flavors, like **mushroom soba** and warm sake to complete trip.

WINTER

The combination of Tokyo's winter illuminations and New Year traditions creates a modern identity. Illuminations as a winter event in Tokyo began to gain popularity in the 1980s, inspired by Western holiday lights and adopted with the Tokyo twist of transforming entire neighborhoods with intricate, large-scale LED displays. **Tokyo Midtown's illuminations** in Roppongi started in the early 2000s as part of the area's development, with Roppongi embracing its identity as a modern art and design district.

The **Shibuya Blue Cave** illumination has also a unique background, with the original installation appearing along the Nakameguro River before moving to Shibuya in recent years. This brilliant blue tunnel effect celebrates Tokyo's contemporary, urban culture, making it one of the most photographed seasonal events in the city. **Odaiba's waterfront** lights, reflecting off Tokyo Bay, highlight the stunning skyline and the Rainbow Bridge, which itself was constructed in 1993 and was originally designed to light up in soft colors to represent harmony.

Tokyo's New Year traditions, on the other hand, are rooted deeply in Japanese Shinto and Buddhist practices that date back centuries. **Hatsumode**, the first shrine or temple visit of the year, is an important ritual where people pray for health, prosperity, and good fortune for the coming year. At famous sites like **Meiji Shrine** and **Senso-ji Temple**, hatsumode has been celebrated for generations; Meiji Shrine, built in honor of Emperor Meiji and Empress Shoken in the early 20th century, attracts millions on New Year's Day alone. Senso-ji, Tokyo's oldest temple founded in **628 AD**, offers a special historical charm, making it a revered place to mark the start of a new year.

Visiting these shrines during hatsumode, you'll notice traditional **osechi ryori** being sold by vendors – colorful foods that each hold a symbolic meaning for good fortune, longevity, and prosperity. Dating back to the Heian period (794-1185), osechi was originally reserved for nobility and has since become a popular treat for the New Year, embodying centuries of tradition.

Illuminations: Mid-November to Early January

The winter lights turn the city into a glowing wonderland, and you'll find some of the best illuminations at **Tokyo Midtown** in **Roppongi, Shibuya Blue Cave,** and **Odaiba.** You can start at **Tokyo Midtown** for a display that fills **Midtown Garden** with bright, colorful LEDs from **5 p.m. to 10 p.m.**. It's free, so head to **Roppongi Station**, take **Exit 8**, and walk straight into the lights. The area can get busy, so get there by **4:30 p.m.** if you want a good view as the lights come on. If it's cold, warm up with hot chocolate from **Bill's Tokyo Midtown** nearby.

Next, go to **Shibuya Blue Cave** along **Shibuya Koen-dori**, which creates a stunning blue tunnel all the way to **Yoyogi Park**. Take **Shibuya Station's Hachiko Exit** and walk a few minutes to see thousands of blue LEDs that stretch for about **250 meters**. The lights are on from **5 p.m. to 10 p.m.**, and weekdays are best if you want fewer people around. Grab a quick hot drink or snack at **Blue Bottle Coffee** or one of the many nearby shops.

For views over **Tokyo Bay**, head to **Odaiba's Rainbow Bridge and Decks Tokyo Beach**. The lights reflect beautifully over the water, and you'll get a view of the whole skyline. Take the **Yurikamome Line** to **Odaiba-Kaihinkoen Station** or **Tokyo Teleport Station** on the **Rinkai Line**. There's a viewing deck at **Decks Tokyo Beach** and cozy seating at **Eggs 'n Things** if you'd rather watch the lights from inside with a snack. The best time to arrive is around **5 p.m.** to walk around before choosing a spot to sit back and enjoy the view.

CHAPTER 9
TOKYO ON A BUDGET

BUDGET-FRIENDLY ACCOMMODATIONS

For affordable yet convenient places to stay, **capsule hotels, hostels, and budget hotel chains** are some of the great options, especially in neighborhoods like **Asakusa, Shinjuku, and Ueno**. In Asakusa, for example, there are capsule hotels right along **Asakusa Dori** near **Senso-ji Temple** that let you experience traditional Tokyo charm at prices around **¥2,000 to ¥4,000 per night**. Just take the **Tokyo Metro Ginza Line** to **Asakusa Station**, and you're a short walk away. Capsule hotels are unique in that they give you a compact sleeping pod, which is surprisingly comfortable and a great way to stay centrally located without spending a lot. You'll share facilities like bathrooms and lockers, so bring a **small lock** for valuables.

Khaosan World Asakusa Hostel is nearby and offers dorms with prices ranging from **¥2,500 to ¥5,000**. This hostel has a kitchen and lounge area, perfect if you enjoy meeting other travelers. You're also just minutes from the bustling **Nakamise Shopping Street**, so it's easy to grab a traditional snack like **melon pan** (a sweet bread) and explore the area on foot. For transit, both the **Ginza and Asakusa lines** stop here, making it easy to reach other parts of the city.

In **Shinjuku**, consider **Nine Hours Capsule Hotel**, conveniently located near **Shinjuku Station**. It's perfect if you're catching the JR Yamanote Line or other major lines. Shinjuku is bustling with affordable food options, especially around **Omoide Yokocho**, where you can find budget-friendly yakitori (grilled chicken skewers) and izakayas (casual Japanese pubs). Staying in Shinjuku costs slightly more, with capsule hotel prices averaging around **¥3,000 to ¥5,000**.

APA Hotels and **Toyoko Inn** have branches in central areas like **Ikebukuro** and **Ueno**. Rooms in these budget chains range between **¥5,000 and ¥8,000** per night and offer a bit more space, a private bathroom, and amenities like free Wi-Fi and, often, a small breakfast. **Toyoko Inn Ueno** is ideal for travelers who want to explore Ueno's cultural spots, like **Ueno Zoo** and the **Tokyo National Museum**. It's near **JR Ueno Station** on the Yamanote Line, providing direct access to popular districts. For food, nearby **Ameya-Yokocho Market** offers cheap, tasty street food options, perfect for a budget-friendly meal after a day out.

To get around smoothly, consider a **Tokyo Metro 24-hour Pass** for **¥600**, giving you unlimited rides on Tokyo's extensive metro system, which can help you save on transit costs when you're hopping around to different parts of the city. You can also find affordable eateries within convenience stores like **7-Eleven, FamilyMart, and Lawson**, where you can pick up onigiri (rice balls), bento boxes, and drinks for less than **¥500**.

NINE HOURS CAPSULE HOTEL

At **Nine Hours Capsule Hotel** in Tokyo, you'll find a sleek, minimalistic experience designed for tourists who want convenience and a unique stay without a high price. Located in busy districts like **Shinjuku** (near Shinjuku Station), **Akasaka** (near Akasaka-Mitsuke Station on the Tokyo Metro Ginza and Marunouchi Lines), and **Hamamatsucho** (close to Hamamatsucho Station on the JR Yamanote Line), Nine Hours offers an ideal setup for getting around easily. If you're at Shinjuku, for example, Shibuya and Harajuku are just a short ride away, making it convenient to dive into nearby shopping and nightlife.

The hotel's **capsules cost between ¥3,000 and ¥5,000 per night** depending on location and season, giving you a budget-friendly option while keeping you in the heart of Tokyo's action. Each capsule is crafted for relaxation and privacy, with adjustable lighting, high-quality bedding, and USB charging points—ensuring you stay connected and comfortable after a long day. Check-in starts at **2 p.m.**, and checkout is at **10 a.m.**; staff provide you with a **key card for capsule access and locker storage**.

Every Nine Hours location keeps things streamlined, with **separate floors for men and women** and shared bathrooms and showers equipped with **shampoo, conditioner, body soap, and towels**—so you don't have to worry about packing toiletries. Need coffee or a quick snack? **Convenience stores and cafes** are usually nearby, and each area has restaurants with options ranging from **sushi** and **ramen** to **donburi** rice bowls, letting you enjoy local flavors just steps from the hotel.

To make the most of your stay at Nine Hours, consider booking ahead for popular dates, as these capsule hotels often fill up fast due to their excellent locations and affordable prices. Additionally, bring a **portable phone charger** for exploring Tokyo's bustling streets all day, and, if you're a light sleeper, **earplugs** can be handy to block out ambient noise.

For transportation, **Shinjuku Station** (JR Yamanote Line) is a convenient hub if you're staying at Nine Hours Shinjuku, offering direct routes to major neighborhoods. From Nine Hours Akasaka, **Akasaka-Mitsuke Station** is a few minutes' walk, connecting you to central Tokyo's metro lines. And if you're at Nine Hours Hamamatsucho, **Hamamatsucho Station** provides easy access to Tokyo's waterfront and central districts via JR lines.

FREE AND LOW-COST ATTRACTIONS

You can start at **Meiji Shrine**, where is located at **1-1 Yoyogikamizonocho, Shibuya City**. It's an easy walk from **Harajuku Station** on the JR Yamanote Line or the Tokyo Metro Chiyoda Line, just head for the giant torii gate, and you're in. Open **from sunrise to sunset**, this serene, wooded spot has no entrance fee, allowing you to immerse yourself in a forest-like setting right in the city. **Nearby in Yoyogi Park**, you can pack a snack from a nearby **FamilyMart or 7-Eleven** for a little on-the-go picnic under the park's cherry blossoms in spring or lush green foliage in summer.

Then head to **Tokyo Metropolitan Government Building** at **2-8-1 Nishi-Shinjuku**. A 10-minute walk from **Shinjuku Station's West Exit**, you can visit the observation deck on the 45th floor for stunning city views for free. The deck is open **from 9:30 a.m. to 11 p.m.** and offers views of Tokyo landmarks like Skytree and even Mt. Fuji on clear days. Arrive early evening to capture both the sunset and city lights without fighting large crowds.

Next, **Senso-ji Temple** in **Asakusa** (close to **Asakusa Station** on the Ginza and Asakusa Lines) lets you experience history in a vibrant setting at **2-3-1 Asakusa, Taito City**. This ancient temple, Tokyo's oldest, is open day and night, so you can visit the grounds whenever suits your schedule. Walk along **Nakamise Street** leading to the temple, where food stalls offer classic Japanese snacks like **taiyaki** (fish-shaped waffles with sweet fillings) and **senbei** (rice crackers) for around **¥100-¥300 each**. Enjoy the sights of the temple without an entrance fee, and try a quiet visit early morning or late evening to avoid the busiest hours.

For a dose of Tokyo's art, stop by **The National Museum of Modern Art (MOMAT)** at **3-1 Kitanomaru Park, Chiyoda City**. **Takebashi Station** on the Tokyo Metro Tozai Line is closest, and the museum often offers free entry on the first Sunday of each month. Wander the galleries showcasing both traditional and contemporary Japanese art, and if you're in the area around noon, visit **Kitanomaru Park** for an afternoon stroll surrounded by seasonal flowers and autumn foliage in November.

Finally, end at **Ueno Park**, a spacious green area located at **Ueno Onshi Park, Taito City**, right next to **Ueno Station** on the JR Yamanote Line. The park is open 24/7, and you'll find various museums nearby if you feel like adding a paid visit to places like **Tokyo National Museum** or the **Ueno Zoo**.

FREE ATTRACTIONS

Head first to **Meiji Shrine** in **Shibuya**, close to Harajuku Station on the JR Yamanote Line or Meiji-Jingumae Station on the Tokyo Metro Chiyoda Line. As you enter through the huge **torii gates**, walk along the peaceful forest path surrounded by over **100,000 trees**. The shrine, built in **1920** to honor Emperor Meiji and Empress Shoken, opens with sunrise and closes at sunset, and it's completely free to visit. Don't forget to stop by the **temizuya**, the water pavilion where you can wash your hands and mouth before praying—a quick way to follow the shrine's traditions. On weekends, you might even see a **Shinto wedding procession**. Afterward, take a quick detour to **Takeshita Street** nearby for crepes or bubble tea, great for a snack before visiting more.

Next, head to **Senso-ji Temple** in **Asakusa**. Take the **Tokyo Metro Ginza Line** or **Toei Asakusa Line** to Asakusa Station. The temple, Tokyo's oldest, was founded in the **7th century**. Enter through **Kaminarimon Gate** with its massive red lantern, and walk down **Nakamise Street**, lined with traditional shops and food stalls selling taiyaki (fish-shaped cakes with sweet fillings), senbei (rice crackers), and more, each costing around **¥100-¥300**. At the main temple, which is open 24 hours (though the main hall closes around **5 p.m.**), join others in a small offering or simple clap-and-pray tradition. Check out the **omikuji** (fortune slips) for **¥100** and get a little bit of insight into your luck. For snacks, Asakusa's famous stalls nearby serve treats like matcha ice cream and melon bread.

For a city view without the cost, go to the **Tokyo Metropolitan Government Building** in **Shinjuku**. From Shinjuku Station, walk about 10 minutes to reach this 243-meter-tall building with **observation decks on the 45th floors** of both North and South towers, which open from **9:30 a.m. to 11 p.m.** (South tower closes earlier, around **5:30 p.m.**). Best times to visit are during sunset for the city views or in the morning for a chance to spot **Mount Fuji**. There's a small café here too, perfect for grabbing a coffee while enjoying the view.

TRANSPORTATION HACKS

To really maximize your Tokyo travel on a budget, you've got options that stretch across **metro, JR, and local free rides** so you're covered from start to finish. Grab a **24-hour Tokyo Metro Pass**, available for about ¥800 at major spots like Tokyo Station, Narita, and Haneda airports. This pass lets you move freely on Tokyo Metro and Toei Subway lines, ideal if you're jumping from vibrant **Shibuya** to the bustling **Asakusa** markets or checking out Shinjuku's nightlife. Head straight to any Tokyo Metro or Toei Subway station, and remember that these metros typically run from around **5:00 a.m. until midnight**, so plan accordingly.

When you're looking to explore beyond central Tokyo, think about the **JR Pass** or **Tokyo Wide Pass**. The **JR Pass**, which covers all JR trains including the Shinkansen, works well if you're eyeing a side trip to **Kyoto, Osaka, or Nikko** along with Tokyo's **Yamanote Line**, which circles key locations. At ¥29,650 for a 7-day pass, it's a solid deal if you're covering a lot of ground beyond Tokyo. If you're staying closer to Tokyo but still want to stretch a bit, go for the **Tokyo Wide Pass** at ¥10,180, which works for **Nikko, Mount Fuji**, and areas within the JR East zone for three days. Both can be picked up at JR East Travel Service Centers in **Tokyo Station** or **Shinjuku Station**.

If you're mostly staying within a single area, look for **free ride zones**, like those around the **Ginza Maru Tetsu Line** for local stops at no extra charge, perfect if you're shopping, eating, or hopping around in central districts. For short, easy transfers, walk or hop on **free ride buses** that loop between certain neighborhoods to save on those brief moves between sights.

To keep track of Tokyo's complex transit system, download **Tokyo Subway Navigation for Tourists** or use **Google Maps** with a Japanese SIM card or Wi-Fi pocket for live updates, directions, and prices in real-time. Try starting early in the day, around **9:00 a.m.**, when trains are slightly less crowded than the rush hour surges that hit between **7:00-9:00 a.m.** and **5:00-7:00 p.m.**

Nearby places to grab budget-friendly eats include the **Konbini** convenience stores, like **Lawson, 7-Eleven, and FamilyMart**, where you can find onigiri, sandwiches, and warm bento boxes for ¥200-¥600.

BUDGET BITES AND CONVENIENCE STORE EATS

To find great food in Tokyo on a budget, visit convenience stores like **Lawson, FamilyMart,** and **7-Eleven.** These stores are everywhere, especially near big stations like **Shinjuku, Shibuya,** and **Asakusa,** and they're open **24/7.** They offer fresh, affordable meals that make it easy to eat well. For a quick snack, grab **onigiri** (rice balls) in flavors like **salmon, tuna mayo,** or **plum** for around **¥100-¥150** each. They're filling, easy to carry, and a classic choice that you'll see many people grabbing on the go.

If you're looking for a full meal, try a **bento box**, which includes rice, a protein like **fried chicken or fish**, and veggies. Bentos usually cost **¥400-¥600** and are stocked up in the mornings and evenings. If you're shopping in the evening, you may even find discounts. To enjoy street food, head to **Asakusa's Nakamise Street** near **Senso-ji Temple** (take the **Ginza Line to Asakusa Station**), where vendors sell **takoyaki** (octopus balls), **yakitori** (grilled chicken), **melonpan** (sweet bread), and **taiyaki** (fish-shaped pastries). These items cost **¥200-¥500** and give you a taste of Tokyo's best snacks.

If you're around **Akihabara Station** on the **JR Yamanote Line**, pop into one of the convenience stores nearby. They have easy options like **soba** and **udon noodles** for **¥300-¥400** that you can heat up in-store. In many locations, you'll find a little spot to eat standing up, as it's common in Japan not to walk and eat at the same time.

For affordable drinks, grab a hot tea or coffee at the store, which helps in winter, and in the summer, a cooling drink is just as popular. You can withdraw cash from ATMs inside these stores, which are usually foreign-card friendly.

CHAPTER 10
FINAL TIPS

WHAT TO BRING FOR EACH SEASON

Spring in Tokyo, as i told you before, late March to early May, is famous for **cherry blossom season.** You'll find temperatures ranging from cool mornings to warmer afternoons, which is why layering is essential. Wear **a light sweater and a rainproof jacket** since Tokyo experiences occasional spring rain. **Comfortable walking shoes** are essential because you'll be out enjoying cherry blossom parks like Ueno Park or Shinjuku Gyoen. Having a **small, foldable umbrella** in your bag can be a lifesaver for surprise showers. Spring also means unpredictable weather changes, so you may want to pack compact layers that can be added or removed throughout the day.

In summer, June to August, Tokyo experiences hot, humid days with temperatures often above 30°C (86°F). **Breathable, light clothes** are key—think airy T-shirts and loose shorts or skirts. A **sun hat** and sunglasses help protect you from the strong sun, while a **refillable water bottle** keeps you hydrated in the intense heat. Tokyo's humidity can feel overwhelming, especially with long days of sightseeing, so it's helpful to carry a **small towel** for sweat, sunscreen, and even cooling patches from convenience stores. For walking, **lightweight shoes** that won't overheat are a must. Summers in Tokyo are lively, with festivals like the Sumida River Fireworks, so pack for both comfort and festival fun.

Autumn, from September to November, brings cool, crisp air and is a great season to explore Tokyo's gardens, such as **Rikugien Garden** and **Meiji Jingu**

Gaien with fiery fall foliage. You'll want a **light jacket or sweater** that's easy to carry. It's ideal for outdoor adventures, with comfortable walking shoes recommended. Rain is less frequent but still possible, so pack a **small umbrella** and a **rain-resistant jacket** just in case. Temperatures drop as winter approaches, so an extra sweater for the evenings can be useful.

Winter, from December to February, brings cold but generally dry weather. Daytime highs can stay around 10°C (50°F) or lower, especially in January. A **warm coat**, **scarf**, gloves, and a hat are essential if you plan to enjoy places like the **Tokyo Midtown** illuminations or New Year's temple visits. **Insulated, sturdy shoes** help keep your feet warm, and layering is key indoors as Tokyo's heating is mild compared to other places. While snowfall is rare, it's good to be prepared for chilly days with warm layers that protect from Tokyo's winter breezes.

EMERGENCY CONTACTS AND SAFETY TIPS

Japan is one of the safest countries in the world, but it's still important to know where to go and who to contact if you need help. **Public safety officers, called "koban" officers**, are very approachable and usually found at small stations in busy areas, so don't hesitate to reach out to them for minor incidents, directions, or to report lost items. These officers often know the area very well, and while not all speak English, they will likely be able to assist or guide you to someone who can.

For health emergencies, **Tokyo has a well-established healthcare system**, and many hospitals in central areas like Shinjuku, Roppongi, and Shibuya cater to international patients. **Tokyo Medical University Hospital** and **St. Luke's International Hospital** are well-known options for visitors who may need more advanced care. Carry your **passport and travel insurance information** because many hospitals will require these for admission, and some may even request payment upfront. It's a good idea to keep your insurance provider's contact info saved so they can assist with any direct billing if needed.

In case of natural events like earthquakes or typhoons, Tokyo has extensive emergency preparedness measures. Most buildings, especially high-rises and hotels, are built to withstand earthquakes. **Tokyo Metro stations and public areas have signs** guiding you to evacuation points and emergency supplies. For real-time alerts, download apps like **Yurekuru Call** (for earthquakes) or **NHK World** to get alerts in English for various weather events or emergencies. **Tokyo Metropolitan Government also offers an English emergency guide**, which you can save on your phone or access at their tourist information centers located in areas like Shinjuku.

Local safety apps, such as Safety Tips Japan, can provide you with weather warnings, safety alerts, and more localized information in English. Knowing basic Japanese phrases can also help if you're in an unfamiliar area, but most urban signs have English translations, especially in transportation hubs. **Having a portable Wi-Fi or SIM card** also allows you to access maps, navigate city areas, and translate phrases in real time, making it easier to stay safe.

Be aware of transportation and station-specific safety tips. For example, **train platforms can be crowded during peak hours,** and platform gates, marked lines, and announcements are meant to guide and ensure safety. Many stations have emergency buttons on platforms if someone falls or drops something onto the tracks, so don't hesitate to use these if you see an accident.

In general, Japan has a low crime rate, but it's still smart to **keep your belongings close in crowded areas** like Shibuya and Harajuku. Pickpocketing is rare but possible, especially in areas where tourists gather. If you lose something valuable, visit the local **koban** and ask about it there, as many lost items are turned in and logged.

Knowing key embassy contacts is also important. Most embassies are in the Hiroo and Roppongi neighborhoods, making it convenient if you lose your passport or need consular assistance. Each embassy has specific operating hours, so it's best to call or email them for exact instructions on what to do if you lose documents.

QUICK RECAP

Make sure you've got your **passport** with at least six months left before it expires, so you don't run into issues. Take a quick picture of the passport's main page, the one with your photo and info, and store a printed copy somewhere in your suitcase and also keep a digital copy on your phone or email. For the **visa**, if you have it on your phone or email, screenshot it so it's easy to pull up if someone asks, just in case Wi-Fi isn't working when you need it.

When it comes to **where you're staying**, don't just rely on the address—save it in Google Maps, because it'll make things much easier if you're offline or in a new area. Double-check the check-in and check-out times so you know if you can go straight there or need to store your luggage somewhere. It's also smart to call or email if you'll arrive late; some places have specific hours for checking in, especially smaller hotels.

If you're using **train passes** like the JR Pass, read up on how to activate it. Usually, you'll need to visit a major station or the airport to get it started. Make sure you have it and your passport handy at the ticket gate since you often need both together. Keep the pass in an easy-to-grab spot in your bag to save yourself from digging around later.

Packing smart makes a difference for the weather. Spring or fall? Bring layers like light jackets or sweaters since mornings can be chilly and afternoons warm. In summer, it's pretty hot, so pack a folding fan, a water bottle, and maybe even a cooling towel; it'll help you stay comfortable while you're exploring. For winter, bring a good coat, gloves, and a hat, as Tokyo gets quite cold, especially when the sun goes down.

Don't forget **power essentials**. Japan uses a 100V plug, which is different if you're coming from outside Japan, so pack an adapter. A power bank is super useful since charging stations aren't common, and it's a lifesaver when you're out for the day. Comfortable shoes are a must since you'll probably walk a lot; adding cushioned insoles can make a big difference. Also, bring a small **first-aid kit** with basics like blister pads, painkillers, any regular medicine you take, and pack it all together so it's easy to grab.

You'll want to keep some **printed travel details**, like your flight information, hotel reservations, and tickets for any sights you're visiting, in a folder or travel organizer with your passport. If you're planning to use digital tickets or passes, download them in advance so they're ready if Wi-Fi isn't cooperating when you need it.

For **daily comfort**, carry a small refillable water bottle since you'll find vending machines all over, and have a small bag ready for essentials. Download some key apps—Google Maps (offline maps are great), Google Translate for quick translations, Japan Official Travel App for transit help, and a weather app focused on Tokyo's forecasts to plan your days better. And don't forget tissues and hand sanitizer; some public bathrooms won't have soap or hand dryers, so it's better to have these on hand.

CONCLUSION

I hope this guide makes your trip smooth and full of great moments. Growing up here, I've seen every part of this city—the temples, the shops, the quiet parks, and the busy, colorful streets. From the crossing at Shibuya to the calm gardens around the Imperial Palace, everything I've shared is based on my own time exploring these places.

As you go around, look out for the little things that make the city unique—the small shrines between skyscrapers, vending machines with every drink you can imagine, and food stalls where you can try something new at every turn. Each neighborhood has its own feel, like the stylish cafes in Harajuku, the traditional markets in Ueno, or the neon lights of Shinjuku at night. The people here might seem reserved, but they're friendly and used to visitors, and a simple thank you, "arigatou," can make a difference.

If you need a break, step into a park, try some local snacks from a convenience store (they're surprisingly good), or take a moment to watch the flow of people—it's all part of the experience. Use the tips and directions here to see the city like a local, whether you're trying street food, finding temples, or just getting around. Enjoy every bit, and make the most of everything this place has to offer.

— *Hana Takashiro*

INDEX

Index

Made in the USA
Las Vegas, NV
28 December 2024

15525648R00069